Camino de la Luna

Unconditional Love

by Pearl Howie

First Edition
Copyright © Pearl Howie 2017
Published by Pearl Escapes
All rights reserved
ISBN 978-0-9956474-3-5
The moral right of the author has been asserted

For my ancestors

It struck me on this journey how I had studied the wisdom of ancient cultures for over 7 years, and despite occasionally being mauled, cut up and disgusted by "healing" practices, I was still open to listening to ancient tribal knowledge…
…yet I was deaf to much of the wisdom of my mother and grandmother, my living antecedents. So I decided to as don Miguel Ruiz would say (the Fifth Agreement)
"Be sceptical but learn to listen."

All of my life I questioned why my parents did what they did, how things worked out, trying to understand, and again, at a certain point of this journey I understood that if "I am perfect and every step I take is perfect" then so is everyone else's, even my parents.

So I apologise for my ignorance, my blindness and my judgement of my ancestors, living and not so living, and I understand that every single step of all of their journeys was perfect, because without them I would not be here.

Thank you, thank you, thank you for my life.

Also by the Author

Books in this Series

Camino de la Luna – Take What You Need (self help/travel)

Closely Related

free Feeling Real Emotions Everyday (self help)

Japan Is Very Wonderful

Other Titles

The Guide to Spa Breaks and Escapes from Pearl Escapes

The Guide to Massage, Spa Treatments and Healing from Pearl Escapes

Meditation for Angry People

The Wee, The Wound And The Worries: My Experience Of Being A Kidney Donor

Love And The Perfect Wave (romantic novel)

Individual regional guides to spas and escapes, including:

Cozumel, Las Vegas, London Spas and Massage, Bath Spa, Swimming With Wild Manatees, Tuscany With Teenagers, The Lake District, Brockenhurst, Iceland, Florida, Key Largo, Orlando, Vero Beach, The Everglades, Clearwater, New York, Paris With Kids, Marrakech, China (Hong Kong, Yangshuo, Shanghai, Huangshan and Beijing), Zadar, Croatia and Barcelona

Video

Everything To Dance For

Contents

Introduction	6
It's A Good Job I Went To The Bank	11
On Just Being Here	14
Having Slept Well In Seattle	18
By The Time You Read This It Will Be Gone	25
I Guess I Picked The Wrong Town To Give Up Coffee	27
Snoqualmie	43
The Silent Mind	45
Stalking and Recapitulation	47
Death Is Just An Illusion, Separation Is Just An Illusion	48
The Wild Iris Inn in La Conner	49
Orcas Island	50
Doe Bay Retreat	52
A Place Has An Energy Or A Personality, A Style	55
Mount Constitution	58
San Juan Island	60
I Realise How Much Of Me	65
How Could I Ever Get Tired Of Ferryboats?	66
Vancouver	76
All The Way Round Seattle	77
Maui	86
The Top Of The Mountain	93
Ha	104
I Let Go	108
Somewhere Over The Rainbow	109
Don't Wait (Part 2)	117
ALOHA	118
Photo Credits	120
About the Author	120
Staylist	121
Book References and Further Reading	122

Introduction

Hello, I'm Pearl and there's a few things you're going to need to know about me if this book is going to make any sense to you. At this point I've realised it is one of a series of books (I wonder whether other writers knew when they began that they'd keep writing in a certain direction, or if they were as clueless as me when they wrote those first ones). You'll see from my list of books "Also by the Author" on page 4 that this is the second in the series, with two other full colour books being closely related or prequels. I've been writing about travel and spas for seven years, and those earlier books are also part of this journey, although they were never intended to be read in any particular order - there's a natural progression; the first spa books had way more detail, then over time the descriptions became broader and the same thing is true of this series of books.

To write properly about spas and massage I had to describe how I felt, because this ultimately, (outside of strictly "beauty" procedures) is the goal, to feel "better". It wasn't easy, and when I look back at things I wrote I see a commonality with incredible writers whose work I love, but whose apologetic "excuse me if I mention a personal feeling, I know it's very introspective" drives me fricking nuts. I apologise for apologising. This is the game we are playing, this being human, this having feelings and I make no apologies for what I joyfully, loudly call "extreme navel gazing". It's my job. For me it is the best, hardest job in the world, I chose it, it chose me, it is mine by inheritance, it is how I was made and I fricking love it, love my life and to echo Rilke, Wilde and Rumi, to celebrate myself, loudly, joyfully and encourage others, teach them to do the same is my utmost joy.

But I've got ahead of myself. Because I wasn't myself for a long time - I had to do some waking up, and this journey through spas and healing, only seven years in some respects, much longer if I trace the sources, to becoming, with all humility, one of the world's experts on spas and traditional healing, was a journey to finding myself, freeing myself from who I had been taught, who I had taught myself to be. A journey ultimately to Aji Spa in Arizona where I woke up to the great pain of not living my own life.

Why on earth would I have done that?

Well, one reason was denial – the first step in the grieving process.

In 2015 I opened the door to a loss I had never allowed myself to fully feel (which I talk about in "free Feeling Real Emotions Everyday" which I wrote after Aji Spa, in 2016).

A few months later, in 2015, I organised a trip for a client to Japan. "Japan Is Very Wonderful" is probably the last of my spa guidebooks – kind of like an "escape in a box" – one hotel, one spa, one restaurant, sometimes threaded together on a longer journey, but I realised this year (2017) I had to finish it because it was a prequel to this series.

Not long before I experienced that profound awakening in Aji Spa I came up with something. I was very proud of it, it came from those seven years of research, from reading pretty much every self-help book out there, from years of therapy, from a lot of break ups, it felt like the very first new thing I could contribute to the world. Not just reporting on spas, not just "journalism" or "memoire" but something inherently true I had discovered, like a mathematical theorum (I have an Honours degree in Pure Mathematics), a tool that could be used by others to get out of their personal hell. It is this:

"Every life is a miracle.

Every love is a miracle.

We are born in love, but then experience loss which causes us pain, pain we can't handle all at once, so we start to numb ourselves. We take the things that were supposed to make our lives better and turn them into addictions, drugs that help us lose ourselves.

We can turn anything into heroin.

We're built to slowly deal with the pain and get over it, come back to our true selves, and we're doing our best but we need help, and too often when we ask for help we ask the wrong people or at the wrong time. And we surround ourselves with people who think they need us to keep acting the same way, like walls we build to lock our fake selves in and keep out the freedom that comes when we recognize our true selves, that we are animals, that we are human, that we are love itself.

All we need to heal is to feel alive, to remember that our life is a miracle.

All we need to feel alive is to follow our heart.

The universe will do the rest."

But it's one thing to have a fabulous theorum. It's another to live it, practice it everyday.

Do I make it sound difficult? Do I make luxury spa treatments and international travel sound arduous?

That's only because it is. Because this is my path to freedom, to releasing emotional poison (to know more about that you're going to need to read some don Miguel Ruiz – resources at the back of the book), to unlearn all the ways I've learned throughout my life to NOT be me. All the beliefs I learned which serve as bars, as walls to keep me acting in a domesticated way. Where I am now on my journey I am having experiences about rehabilitating wild animals. It's teaching me a lot, but it was also something that touched me on my very first day of being me, after waking up in Aji Spa, visiting Bearizona near the Grand Canyon, when I realised the wrong turn I took a week before was not a wrong turn but my heart leading me there, to learning that when bears have been in captivity they have to be taught to be wild again, to stop pacing back and forward even when they are in the forest.

It takes time, and requires great compassion and patience with oneself (and all the people that try to put you back in your box) to learn to be free, wild again.

It's hard to keep it in order, because the more I travel the more things echo, lessons I need to learn over and over again, lessons I need to learn differently, on a deeper level, practices that served me at one point which I need to let go of for the next stage.

Just when I think I know what's going on I realise I am a beginner, that I need to constantly be striving to have a beginner's mind, an empty cup, yet also a surety, a faith in what I have learned so I do not lose hope or my way too far.

Life changed drastically after writing "free…" and the P.S. to that book was really the Prologue to the next one - "Camino de la Luna – Take What You Need" which starts in November 2016 when I left my flat in London, sold my home of 22 years and went on the Camino de Santiago in Spain, terrified.

So now a spoiler (don't read this if you want to read "Camino…" and enjoy it fully), on that journey I learned how to sleep in hostels, how to wash my clothes in the shower, carry my life on my back walking from dawn to dusk, and then give it up because it actually costs more than all faster methods of travel because you need to pay to eat more and sleep more the slower you travel. I sort of became a digital nomad and I got over a lot of fears. I thought the book ended when my Camino ended, when I got back into my life, but I realised as an annoying bar sign said "The real Camino begins when you finish." Going home was a spiritual test, and then my spiritual retreat in Mexico over New Year was more of a family vacation (although there was some hard work in there too).

I learned to live much more simply than the places I had stayed over the years, but I also realised that my previous trip to Mexico, in July 2015 had been a test or training for everything else, dealing with bugs and heat and sunburn too.

When I went wrong and got sidetracked, the universe or God (for me it's God but you can sub in the universe should you choose or whatever symbol you like for this wisdom that seems to guide me – my subconscious if that's the way your philosophy lies), guided me back, because I kept asking it to, and so I ended up in Baja, Mexico looking for whales, grey whales to be specific, and I found them. I found love.

Not boy girl love (that's the way I'm inclined), but I experienced how much whales love us, and I hugged and kissed one (and put my hand in her mouth and then found it was not recommended). And none of it would have been possible if I hadn't learned everything I learned, followed the yellow shells to Finisterre in Spain, and then discovered yellow shells at "The Halfway Inn" in Baja. So I learned to trust and not be afraid, more and more of the time.

So I believe in magic. The mystical. I would describe myself as a mystic, which surprises the hell out of me because, although I've always been a Christian, I've also always been as pragmatic as the majority of Christians I've met. Not so anymore. While my Christian faith is stronger than ever, and I am more curious about the deep mysteries of Christ, my Buddhist understanding is also deeper, stronger, my Sufi experiences more dreamlike and jolly, silly, insanely fun and I believe in the deep wisdom of Judaism (Jesus quite liked it I understand) and ancient cultures.

There's also a load of bollocks. And corruption. Including people trying to fleece you for money, get you into bed, get you to keep your knickers (and the rest of your clothes) on and generally control you mind, body and spirit.

Remember that many cultures and religions have embraced slavery, stoning, FGM, forced marriage, honour killings, damning class systems, the abolition of women's and other "lesser beings" rights. It's not nice. I happen to think it's stupidity or insanity.

Perhaps the best question when asked to do anything by anyone is "does this free you or imprison you?" It's not always easy to answer, so I trust my heart (and you know remember I am a guest in another's home, hotel, temple or country).

Anyway, I digress, the point of this bit is just to fill you in, so you know there are other books if you want to start at the beginning, but if you want to dive in here that's cool too, I'll try not to put so many references in to my previous experiences that I lose you.

I'll do my best.

Let's go.

Lots of love, x P

It's A Good Job I Went To The Bank

Although it felt wrong as I took Mexican pesos out in La Paz, (and shortly I realised I needed to leave Mexico), it was a good job I had the cash, because the last flight that'd get me to a connecting airport for Hawaii had already left La Paz, so the only two options that day (I didn't want to go to LA because of the air pollution) were Seattle or Vancouver out of Los Cabos - a US$200 taxi ride. Seattle was tight, Vancouver an hour later. Vancouver would do, a lot of people told me how nice it was, but Seattle was where my heart lived (and Meredith and Derek and all the characters from "Grey's Anatomy").

So we drove like stink around the mountains of Baja, (me thinking "Hmm, I really should have spent more time enjoying the mountains while I was here.") seeing a little blow from humpback whales on the west coast
and just loving Mexico but desperately hoping I'd make the flight.
I'm not sure my taxi driver had ever actually been to this airport,
he seemed confused, and dropped me off at the wrong terminal.

I had to run with my rucksack across the parking lot to the international terminal, where I found out that yes, I had just enough time for the Seattle flight and yes, I'd have to pay another US$25 for my bag and yes, I ran through security (pissing off the guy strolling along who felt I'd cut him up - "I'm sure I was first.") and was suddenly sitting on a plane bound for Seattle in January in my T-shirt and shorts.

I smiled the whole flight.

The guy at US Immigration did not smile.

All my answers were wrong.

"Where are you going?"

"I don't know. Well, probably Hawaii but I'm going to spend a few days here. Probably."

"Where are staying?"

"I don't know."

"How much money do you have?"

"About ten dollars."

He looked at me blankly. "How are you planning to pay for anything?"

"Oh, I have credit cards. Sorry, I thought you meant exactly how much cash."

"What are you going to be doing in Hawaii?"

"I don't know."

"You do know that you're meant to have a departing flight from the US?"

"Oh really, no sorry I didn't know that."

Then he proceeded to ask me something about Hawaii which I assume is really dirty or illegal because I don't know what it meant. "Sorry I don't know what that is."

"Okay, don't worry. Just go."

"No really, what does it mean, I'm curious?"

"If you were going to do it you'd know what it was. Go on." He practically shoved me into the US. (I refuse to Google it, it might be really nasty.)[1]

1   I just overheard someone; it's WOOFing – Working On Organic Farms, not dirty at all – or at least not that kind of dirty.

I discovered, as I sat in SeaTac airport trying to use the WiFi and then giving in and using my Vodafone WorldTraveller (£5 a day per country), that accommodation in Seattle was on a par with Cancun sandwiched between New Year and the BPM Festival – luckily there was a lot of choice, but it was expensive. I settled on an airport hotel – the Sleep Inn for about $100 because it was already 9pm.
I threw on some more clothes and got the free shuttle bus (which took ages – I should have taken a cab), and then slept 12 hours without my headphones because it was blissfully quiet, with only the rain singing me to sleep.

On Just Being Here

I was sitting in a park one day enjoying the weather when a woman walked past with her toddler and presumably the child's grandfather. The toddler was in raptures, babbling away and running up to her grandpa and hugging him. And the mother said "That's all you have to do to be loved, just be here."

We are
constantly surrounded by love;
the universe's love for us, our love
for ourselves and our deep, deep love
for everyone and everything on the planet.
I know we repeat it so often in Christianity,
it's obvious when a child is born,
when we hold the hand
of one we love
when they're sick,
and yet we forget it so easily.

I am here.

My presence is a blessing to you and your presence is a blessing to me, even the time we make for a cup of coffee. When I walk into the square in Zadar, Croatia I am surrounded by people who have stopped, to take the time for a coffee with a friend, a sister, a colleague. As a local joked to me "Tourists come here and see us all having coffee and say - who does any work?" When I walk into the square in Zadar I am overwhelmed in the presence of so much love. Taking the time to stop and be with each other, or even ourselves, like the Italian "dolce vita" – sweet life, or "la bel far niente" – the beautiful for nothing, as described by Elizabeth Gilbert in "Eat, Pray, Love".

I write this sitting at breakfast at a shabby chic wedding hotel in Cernobbio on the banks of Lake Como in Italy (almost Switzerland), where my body is overjoyed at every bite I eat because I have been suffering a stomach bug for four days.

I have been blessed with a picture window so I can lie in my bed
and see the full moon rise over the lake
and the sun rise
and with the one sun lounger they kindly put out by the pool for me
so I can also lay down in the open air between naps.

At times I have not wanted to be here, even not wanted to be alive,
I have beaten myself up with all the things I might have done to avoid
this and all the things I should be doing and places I want to go.

But I am here, and this morning when I drank my coffee,
when I was able to drink my coffee I cried with the pure joy of it.

I want to be everywhere (well, not quite everywhere).

I want to do everything.

I want to be with all my family, all my friends and
I also want to be alone.

We are blessed with an extraordinary and wonderful buffet of life and this year I have set myself free to go wherever I want, do whatever I want. I have emptied out my life and created the time and money to do it and still I can make it hell. I can torture myself, or I can enjoy the blessings of each moment, even if it is just a respite from lying on the bathroom floor. Yes, having control of my bodily functions is heaven.

Once I was talking to a wonderful lady in my class who had a degenerative disease. She told me "When I can no longer control my bowels, that's when I'm going to Switzerland." (for euthanasia).

I'd just come back from a really bad stomach bug. "I crapped myself twice last week."

Luckily this bug hasn't been that bad (I had one really close moment walking through the village, luckily there was a public (squat!!!) toilet but I made it).

I realised as I made my way around Italy I was following in the footsteps of so many great writers; Rilke, Shakespeare, Byron, Keats, Shelley, Hemingway, Wilde and, here, D.H. Lawrence, who reportedly came to the Italian lakes for one day and ended up staying six months. "Did he have a stomach bug too?" I asked myself as I lay in bed.

Having Slept Well In Seattle

I was super excited to explore. It felt like coming home, although I'd never been anywhere in north North America other than New York, which is another world. I'd discovered from LA, Malibu, Florida and the Florida Keys just how different US places can be, but as I'd topped out in Mexico on not speaking Spanish, figuring out public transport and even the heat, Seattle in January felt like my kinda town. And I was assured of one thing at least; there would be Starbucks. (Although I always try to use local coffee shops, I figured in Seattle that was Starbucks.)

I wanted to explore the city centre and saw a hostel right across from Pike Place and some apartments to rent there too, so I shouldered my rucksack and headed down on Seattle's great airport shuttle train to check it out and, more importantly for a "Grey's" fan, to ride a ferryboat.

There's so much to love about Seattle; the vintage buildings, the seafront, where a sea lion popped up to say hello, but the first thing I learned in Seattle was that this town's homeless people were nothing like those I'd passed so far on this trip.

In Porto I learned from the hostel hotties "the homeless people here are never going to bother you, we need tourists too much"…

…in Seattle, my first encounter with a guy I assumed to be homeless was avoiding his yelling and swearing.

I was not in Kansas anymore (or Portugal, Mexico, or anywhere in Europe). Now I had to be more aware; this was new territory.

So I was cautious as I approached the hostel, but with shared female dorms for $30 it was a good budget option and I was hoping to make new friends, either guests or the hosts.

On the one hand it was perhaps the most organised place I'd ever visited, rules and notices everywhere on the storage of food ("No food in the bedrooms!)

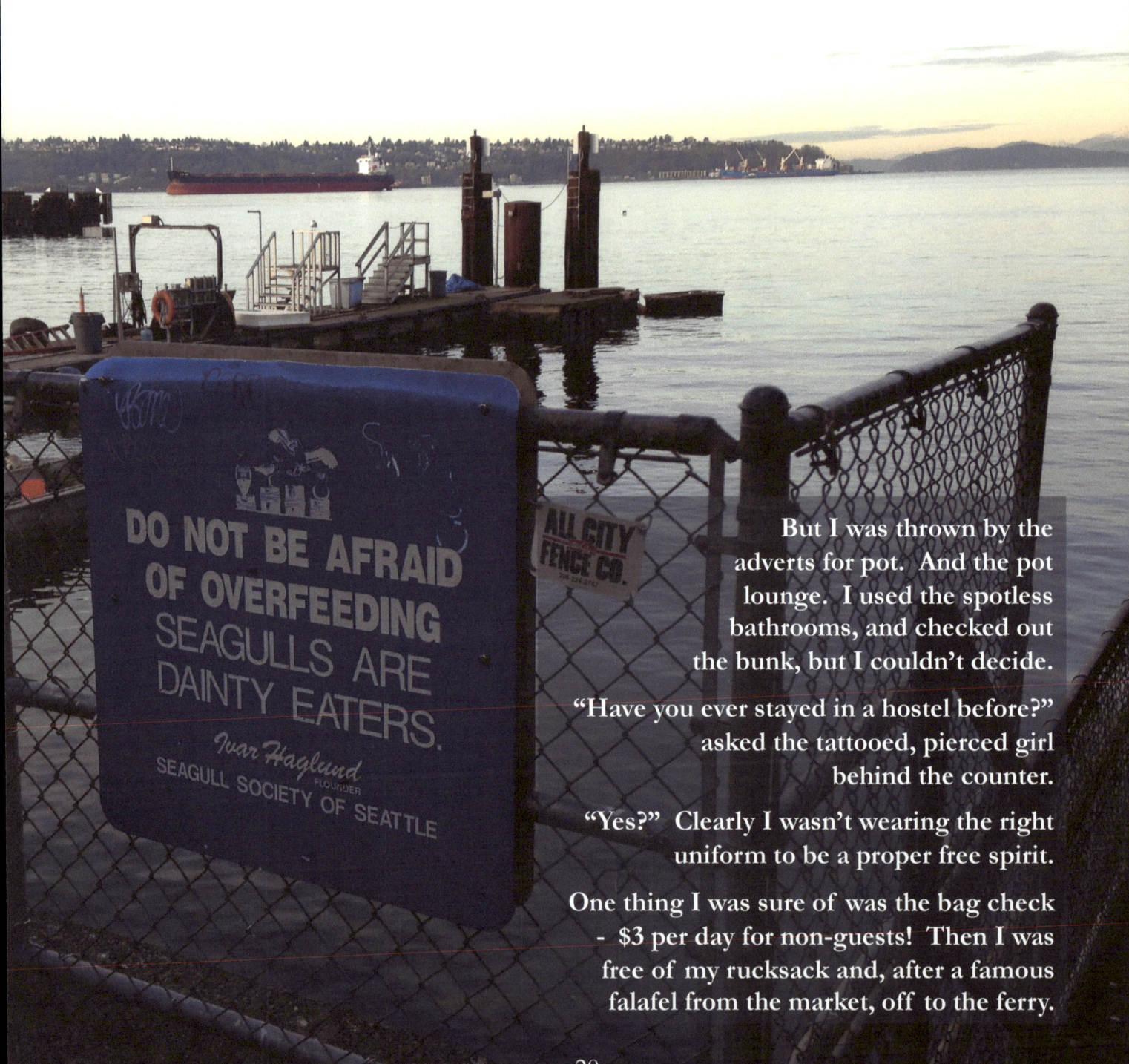

But I was thrown by the adverts for pot. And the pot lounge. I used the spotless bathrooms, and checked out the bunk, but I couldn't decide.

"Have you ever stayed in a hostel before?" asked the tattooed, pierced girl behind the counter.

"Yes?" Clearly I wasn't wearing the right uniform to be a proper free spirit.

One thing I was sure of was the bag check - $3 per day for non-guests! Then I was free of my rucksack and, after a famous falafel from the market, off to the ferry.

For me, a "Grey's Anatomy" fan, riding the ferry boat was a religious experience.

I didn't stop crying the whole time.

The words kept sounding in my head

"Derek's dead."

"Derek's dead."

"Derek's dead."

I was so glad I'd come to Seattle.

I needed to do this.

I had no idea what Bainbridge would be like, I'd just jumped on the first ferry. The terminal was pretty grim – it was clear there were a lot of homeless people sheltering there, using the washrooms, it wasn't a fun place to hang out. I'd better get my act together - come right back on the ferry and find a place to sleep.

Although… it felt rude not to at least get off the ferry and have a wander.

I might as well have a walk, though I wasn't much in the mood. I walked along the river, past the boats and came to Bainbridge.

Where I fell in love.

It was small town America as I dreamed…

The lady in the knitting and outdoors shop, sharing tales of CYCLING with her husband around Baja, Mexico and those bumpy, winding roads and how once they had to keep on going two, three times as long as they'd planned because there just wasn't anywhere to stop.

The older man who asked if I was lost, and told me about the buses and the lodge up the street. And I sat in the café and used the town's free WiFi to look at hotels, mostly all booked up, and I read the leaflets for all the things I love "Yes, I'm home."

But I couldn't settle, not at the lodge, or the chain hotel; full on booking.com "Well, we keep a few rooms, we don't want to have to turn people away." and I was back on the ferry without having had dinner in one of the homely places, because I really ought to find somewhere to sleep before too late.

And I forgot to take a single photo.

By The Time You Read This It Will Be Gone

I went to Tulum, the famous spiritual destination in the Yucatan Mexico, but couldn't find my spot; I checked out a luxury apartment which I couldn't settle on and next door I couldn't even book a pop up tent or a concrete tube to sleep in. I'd be lying if I said there weren't hostel beds, but nowhere that felt right. The music was playing loud, the bars were numerous and I wondered if I'd missed the boat. Was Tulum already gone?

I have a theory about the spiritual places that call us. First come the people who can feel it, feel the pull with their own heart and it's magical and their spirit makes the magic even more powerful because it chimes with the earth and the trees and the ocean waves. But you see, those of us who are sensitive to these vibes, we've also hurt ourselves, been hurt, and we're tempted, perhaps more than people who are asleep to the stuff around them, to block it all out, with alcohol and drugs and other addictions. I don't know if we naturally have different levels of sensitivity, or if it's how open we are each day?

Whether we come because we feel it, or because we hear about it from others, we come, in part, for healing and we come dragging all of our baggage and our demons and our addictions with us. And slowly that once pure spiritual place becomes polluted with fear and drugs (including judgment and intolerance) until it's no longer safe for anyone.

It's like rehab - if it's not run well, if there aren't strong boundaries for what substances and behaviors are allowed, it becomes a place for further abuse, not healing. As Iggie Pop said in the one interview I've read with him, he went to rehab and got offered pills in the hot tub, so had to get out and go it alone.

Many times I felt like I was in rehab, trying to let go of fear, judgment, anger, intolerance, and even regular substances like alcohol, meat, dairy and I decided in the end it wasn't judgmental to say "No, I don't want to be around a bunch of stoned people."

Plus, you know, the last room back at the hostel in Seattle with the pot lounge was booked by the time I checked again.

But if I hadn't "spun" between staying in Bainbridge and heading back to the mainland I would have never seen the waterfront lit up like this as I crossed back over to downtown Seattle, to "the Emerald City".

I was falling in love with the whole Washington area, and despite the rough edges I was also drawn back to downtown.

I Guess I Picked The Wrong Town To Give Up Coffee

I could afford to be blasé in Seattle, I knew where The Sleep Inn was.

…but I wanted to give downtown a go, so I found a discounted top rated hotel, booked it, picked up my rucksack from the hostel (stopping to flaunt my bargain – a single room at the hostel was pricey). I walk over, check in to raised eyebrows but friendliness, check the room – a New York style miniature, (the TV seemed bigger than the bed), ask them to turn off the fridge light shining the Coke brand in my face and please change the sheets (I'm very nice about it… "I'm sure they're clean, I just don't like brown stains in the middle of the sheets.")

…although I don't figure out that that weird noise all night is the elevator until the next morning.

And then I'm off to walk around the Space Needle, (not entirely sure it was the best idea at night) and then back to find a vegan sushi restaurant with a happy hour and to be treated to the unforgettable sight of a homeless woman dropping her pants to take a dump outside all of the posh shops where the hotel is.

Seattle's homeless situation is like nothing I've ever experienced.

The Roosevelt US$121 without breakfast

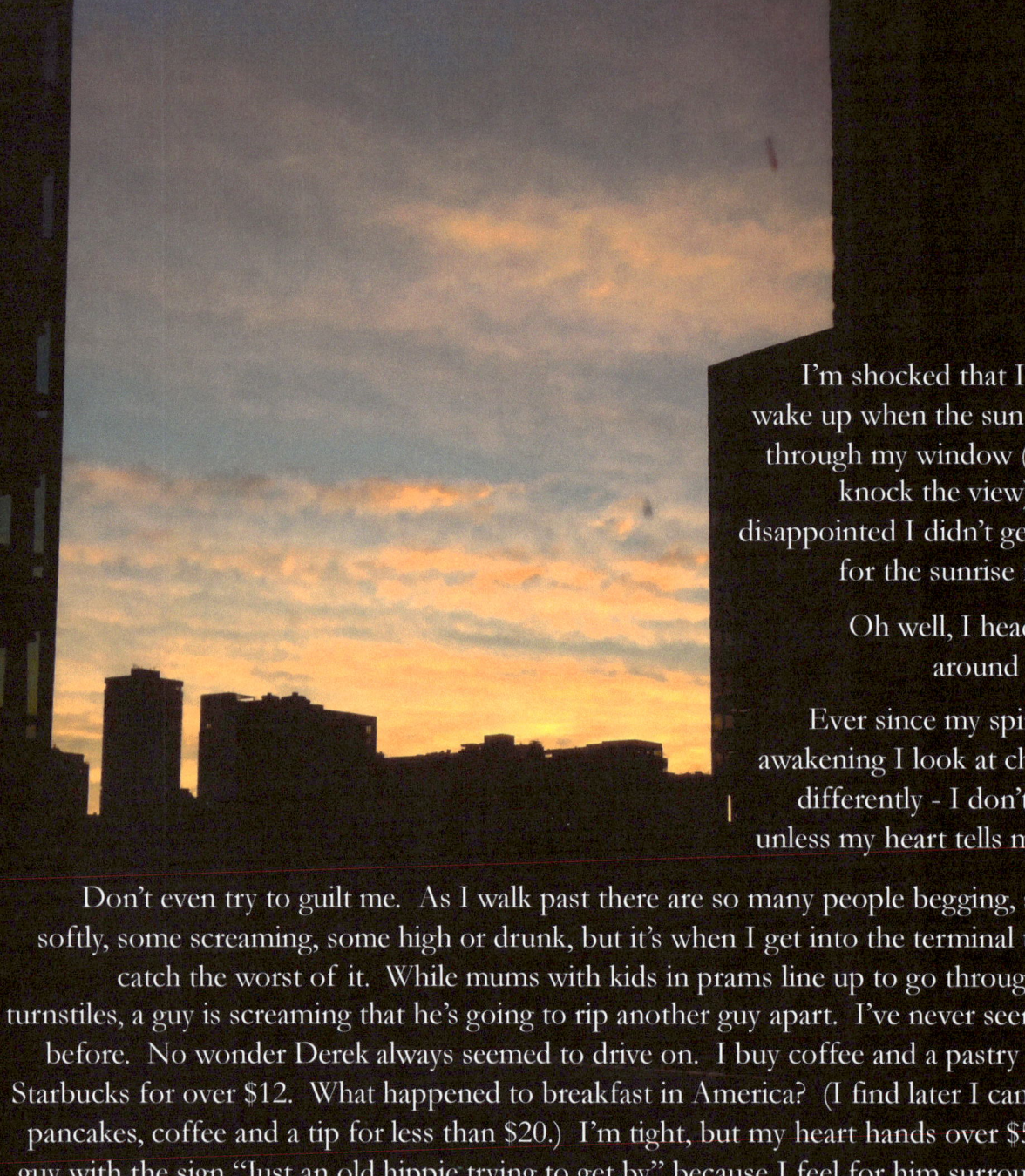

I'm shocked that I only wake up when the sun rises through my window (can't knock the view) and disappointed I didn't get out for the sunrise ferry.

Oh well, I head out around 9am.

Ever since my spiritual awakening I look at charity differently - I don't give unless my heart tells me to.

Don't even try to guilt me. As I walk past there are so many people begging, some softly, some screaming, some high or drunk, but it's when I get into the terminal that I catch the worst of it. While mums with kids in prams line up to go through the turnstiles, a guy is screaming that he's going to rip another guy apart. I've never seen this before. No wonder Derek always seemed to drive on. I buy coffee and a pastry from Starbucks for over $12. What happened to breakfast in America? (I find later I can't get pancakes, coffee and a tip for less than $20.) I'm tight, but my heart hands over $5 to a guy with the sign "Just an old hippie trying to get by" because I feel for him surrounded by the guys off their heads. I gotta get out of downtown Seattle. It's not safe.

It's worth it.

The clouds clear enough to give the most incredible views in every direction.

Strangers come up to me to point out yet another mountain. They're so excited, it's hardly ever visible.

The Olympic Mountains are crystal clear behind Bainbridge.

I would never have seen this if I'd stayed there (cosy as it would have been).

It's so beautiful that I have to stay on the ferry as it turns back around and finish my morning boat tour (plus my check out time is looming).

It's one of the cheapest and most exceptional scenic tours I've ever done (although it's hard to beat any ferry boat ride in the Yucatan).

I want to explore more in Seattle, I've seen there's the REI flagship store – I gotta go there, it may be time to try camping (hotels here are sooooo expensive) and besides, my new laptop decided to crash on the flight from Mexico – I may have lost my book (well, since the last back up) so I need to go to the Apple store. I walk into the YWCA but unlike the one I see advertised in Vancouver this looks hardcore, so many signs warning that you'll get kicked out if you abuse staff. It's not for me, so I go back to my elegant hotel to use the top notch bathroom to warm up.

I'm lucky Seattle has fabulous public transport - buses, trams and ferries, oh my…

And a quick detour through the college campus along the way to the Apple store and I find the cheapest and tastiest meal I've had in the States so far. Thank heavens for college vegans.

Turns out according to the Geniuses at Apple I've overloaded PowerPoint with my first Camino book.

I feel like Captain Kirk. "The system canna' take it!" I'll find a way.

I'm exhausted as they run my back up (and show themselves not to be quite such Geniuses when they keep offering to give me a charging cable - my laptop only has one USB port which is already taken up by the backup drive). We finally get there.

…and it's dark again by the time I make it back to my elegant hotel to pick up my rucksack and realise that the place I've booked to stay, in a "quiet, clean and comfortable room" is right back where I've just come from, although it looks like I'll be slightly better off getting there on the bus.

Except that it's rush hour. Despite the generally wonderful vibe of Seattle where people are friendly and kind, this bus journey is a different kind of hell. "How did I ever travel every day for two hours in this?" I ask myself. The driver keeps yelling at us, to move down, to take off rucksacks (that'll be me then) which is an extraordinarily exhausting balancing act, one hand on the strap, the other on my bag and then at one point threatens to stop the bus because of an argument he sees on his video camera. It's horrible, thank God tomorrow is Saturday.

I jump off the bus in a cold, dark parking lot. I do not like this. It's not even 8pm but it's unpleasant, luckily a kind person (Seattle is full of them) tells me I need to get back on the same bus and keep going a few more stops. When it comes it's a pleasant change and I ride the bus to the closest stop and then walk. Which I hate.

I've walked everywhere, but now it's cold and it's dark and there are nothing but cars, and I realise to get where I need to go I need to walk further up and across the highway bridge – there's no crossing. It's the end of the road for me walking in the States I decide. Tomorrow I hire a car, besides I want to head up to the San Juan Islands, maybe Snoqualmie Falls and it seems almost impossible without a car.

I finally find my house, it's a lovely neighbourhood and thank God, there are trees here, but I have no way to get into the house – luckily there's a guy there who opens the door and I can call my host and figure out that I should have had a text from him with codes to a key safe by my door. There are a hundred rules and regulations, including which of the shared bathrooms I can use, but my room is cute, comfy (if cold) and there is a stunning kitchen which I'm allowed to use, and the heat is on in the entrance, come dining room/kitchen. I'm a little wary with my ghost host…

…but it turns out it's like staying in a hostel for hermits. If I do sight another (single male) guest (as they all seem to be) we mostly just nod. I don't even hear the guy using the bathroom next to me – just notice if the door is locked. And the shower is superb, enough to warm up my chilled bones. And it's lucky that the heater on the wall is the same as at our retreat in Teotihuacan in Mexico (that me and my room mate didn't discover until the last night), so I can turn it on and pass out for a deep 12 hours rest.

The next morning I can't bring myself to leave, especially as I have REI in my sights (and someone already brewed a big pot of coffee for us in the kitchen). I can't contact my host, so just do a repeat booking on booking.com and hope it's okay that I leave everything in my room. Then it's off for the bus and breakfast because I ate my reserve porridge oats for dinner.

Riding the bus back to the centre of town I see tents staked out on the main road's embankments. It's January. People here are desperate; this is not somewhere for me to stay long, I don't want to be taking up a room where there are so few affordable ones.

It's one of those times when my job is simple; eat, sleep and kit up for the next step – whatever that may be. I pass an interesting looking place – The Recovery Café and feel myself duck inside. Next door are all kinds of Anonymous meetings where everyone is welcome, but the sweet guy on the door takes the time to talk me through and help me understand what's going on in Seattle. Their rule is simple, you have to be clean of your drug for three days before you can take part in the activities here. I get it. (And I love that on the first page of their schedule is a talk about don Miguel Ruiz's "The Four Agreements".) As I continue my journey I'll find myself in conversations with people who desperately want help, desperately want answers, but with a glass of red wine in hand they can't drink in anything I'm saying.

We talk about the pot in the hostels and the attitude "It's legal."

"So's tequila." we say at pretty much the same time.

A guy he knows drops in, he's just been to an AA meeting next door, he's shaking, maybe in withdrawal, the guy who runs it shakes his hand, hands him the programme. "Three days" he says, the guy nods, he knows the rules, he's got clean before, he knows what he's doing. The guy who runs the place comes back to me, he wants to give people a chance, not a hand out. It's tough love. But it also keeps the space safe for other people in recovery, he's walking a difficult path. It's a place I'd want to come to if I was in trouble.

I'm shaking myself as I reach REI. I'm glad I've booked the next night in my hostel/house, this is a big deal for me. I had no idea their flagship store was even in Seattle until I read some stuff from the airport, but after watching "Wild" I went to their website to read up on rucksacks before my Camino (they taught me online how to put on a rucksack properly).

In Mexico I was so close to signing up for a beach camping retreat, so close to buying a $50 pop up tent in the camping store there… I feel like a tent is the next step for me.

There's an actual ranger station in the middle of the store, so I spend forever getting maps and information and pissing off the ranger by interrupting because I'm so enthusiastic. He tells me off, and tells me where I can go without special snow gear on a car. "Now is not the time for you to camp." He's pretty definite.

I want to find out about the tribes, but he shakes his head. There are one or two visitor centres, but nothing else he tells me. I see the reservations and the Native American names marked on the maps, the culture all seems so tantalisingly close and yet out of reach.

Then I just walk around, I'm scared to ask for help. My ego is freaking out again.

"You can't do this. You can't do camping." I know I'm not a natural. I go upstairs to walk around the socks.

A friendly guy asks if I need any help. "Yes, is the coffee here any good? I'm freaking out and I need caffeine."

He smiles, and directs me across the street to an artisanal coffee shop – where I hunker down and go through all my usual practices – "I will trust and not be afraid", "I am life passing through my body and if anything happens to me I'm just going back to life." "May life protect me from my self." "I am the rider, my mind is the horse." And I finally find enough calm and confidence to walk back in.

I'm pretty sure I need a sleeping bag. I have an army one which was donated to me for my Camino but I left it behind when I came to Mexico. I've been okay, but it was pretty cold in Teotihuacan and in Guerrero Negro – the desert, at night. It's much colder here.

The guy knows all about sleeping bags, I just don't like his answers. If I want a light one it has to be down, but it's useless if it gets wet. We look at the women's ones, it makes sense to get one that fits properly, and one with a "hood" as that's where you lose the heat, but they all have these foot things so you can't zip them open and use them flat, and sometimes I just want it underneath me. They're also ridiculously expensive. It's good I didn't have to buy one for my Camino when I was so broke, it was nylon, not down, but it did the job. These seem to be $300 minimum. I feel for the homeless people here.

I've heard you can get a sleep liner and it'll give you an extra 5 degrees of heat, but he shakes his head. I look at tents, but they're a ridiculous price - $700 for a small one! I like the look of the shelter things - I saw in a book this is the kind of thing the Cree use so they can have a fire and not smoke out a tent. He looks at me like I'm nuts. I get it a lot.

I don't feel good about it, but I have my $300 sleeping bag in hand. Then I see another assistant. "Yes" she says, "I love my sleep liner, it gives you extra warmth, and you can use it in a hostel if you're not sure about cleanliness. You can get a nylon one or even a silk one, they're pricey but worth it."

I keep telling myself to follow my heart, it loves the silk liner but not the sleeping bag. And then I see it.

My Puffy.

It's right on the end of an aisle – not a sleeping bag, but a down blanket. It's not cheap, nearly $200 but it makes my heart sing, and I'm ditching the sleeping bag and heading to the till… where neither of my cards will work.

Which is a good thing, as I double check the total (which seemed kind of high) and they'd been charging me for a double instead of a single (a difference of $100). So they figure it out while I call up to unfreeze my cards and am told "No, they should work".

Which, of course, when we try again, they do.

I have just enough time to hit Whole Foods, freak out about my bank balance and get more supplies. (I got a weird veggie camping dinner from REI for $11 – just one). I get stuff I can eat cold in case that beautiful kitchen at the house isn't really functional. It's funny, all of my childhood holidays were either staying at my grandparents or camping in the woods (usually with the tent set up by my Grandad) but it's a world away from REI. Camping food was beans and potatoes cooked over the gas stove, and the tents and sleeping bags were never new, only inherited.

There's something wonderful about Seattle, I love riding home on the bus seeing all the neighbourhoods, it's so hard to leave. But tonight I get to curl up, eat my cold dinner (the kitchen's amazing but there are only a few enormous pots), finish downloading "The Big Blue" which I tried to do in Mexico, curl up in my room, under my Puffy (I still need the heater on) and luxuriate in my comfort zone and a movie about free diving. Which I seem to have downloaded in French with English subtitles.

(But I actually do speak French.)

The next morning it's a struggle to leave my cocoon, this comfy room. Nobody bothers me, there's a good hot shower, a kitchen, it's affordable, it even has a laundry room so I can dry my stuff. It's a kind of heaven. The WiFi is excellent and elves come in early and make coffee (or I can if no one else is about). Around the corner is a small wood where I can go hug trees. And it's Sunday.

It's time to go. I want to see the San Juan Islands – I know it's not the season for orcas but I've been lucky so far on this trip with wildlife. I need to get to Anacortes to catch the ferry and I don't think there's a bus.

I pack up my room, dragging my ass, I finish around about check out time and sit in the living room trying to book my car hire. The price goes up before my eyes, maybe it's because it's on the day, because I add insurance, but I can't seem to find a way around it and it ends up about $50 a day. I'm really struggling to press the button, I've got so used to taking buses, trains, even planes and Uber. I've rented cars in the States, in Mexico, in the UK before, but my ego has me spinning, as I sit on my laptop in the living room and the people who run the house finally appear and start cleaning.

"I can do this, I can do this, I can do this."

I finally rent the car from the airport and shoulder my rucksack, which is so heavy with my extra supplies, and hike to the bus stop. Along the way I see an old woman sitting in the middle of the lane heading onto the main road, she has a sign, she's begging. She looks homeless.

I'm struggling the whole way to pick up the car, with myself. I also get really low blood sugar, so stop to eat some trashy food in the airport, which is when I see little birds flying around. This life inside gives me hope.

I get the car. I love how they do it in the States, they just point me to a row of cars and say "Take your pick." One of my wonderful Mexican friends from my retreat in Teotihuacan was a red head, she's the one I'm most in touch with, she lives in Texas.

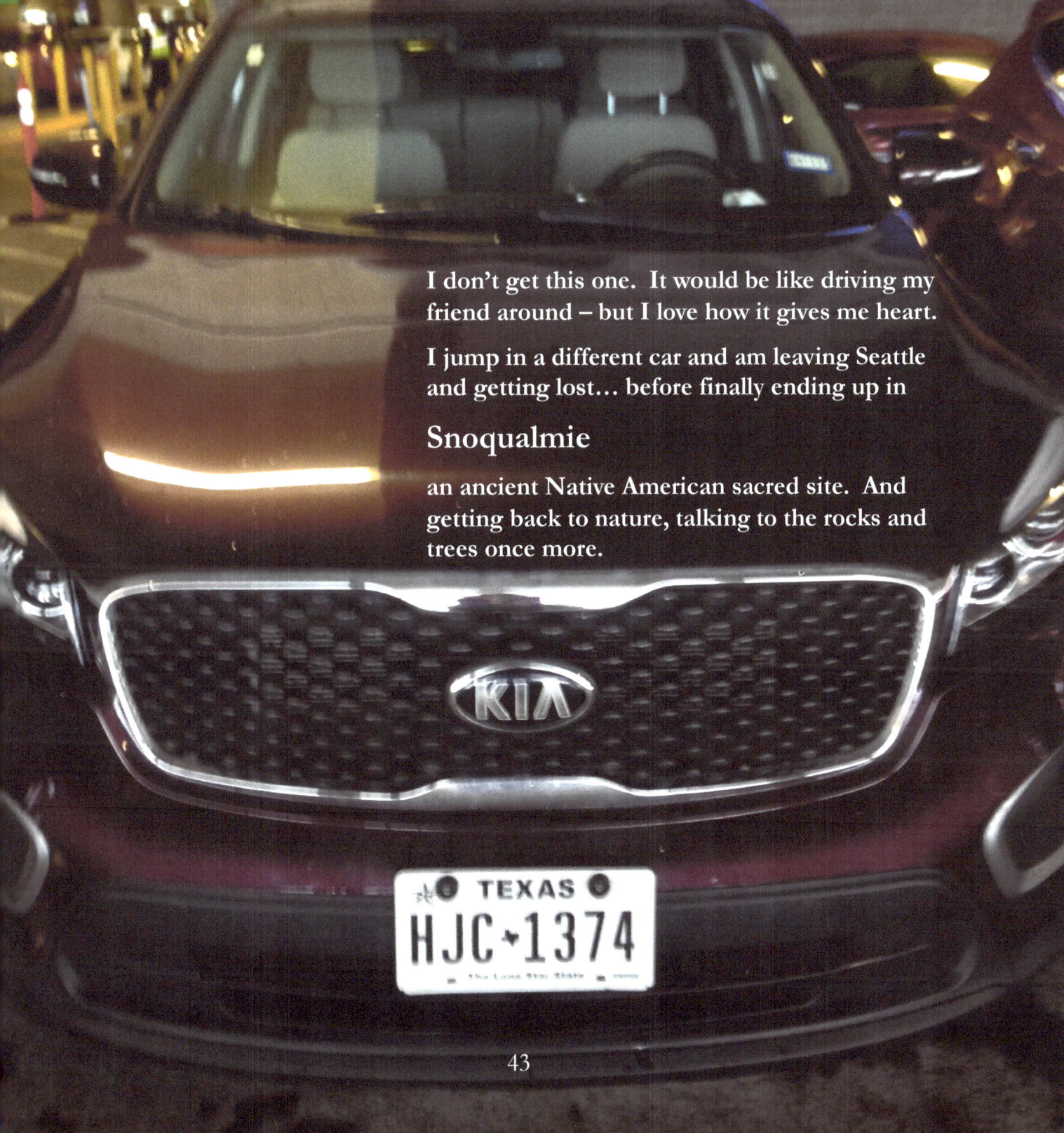

I don't get this one. It would be like driving my friend around – but I love how it gives me heart.

I jump in a different car and am leaving Seattle and getting lost… before finally ending up in

Snoqualmie

an ancient Native American sacred site. And getting back to nature, talking to the rocks and trees once more.

It's such a beautiful place… but the falls have been "civilised", there's a huge power station here for the electricity they draw off the energy of the waterfall.

It's controversial, especially for the Native American people…

…this is a sacred place for them, for anyone who appreciates nature and beauty. It reminds me of Penhas Douradas in Portugal where the rocks had a powerful energy.

Signs around the falls tell the story, ask the question, is it right for the falls to be used this way?

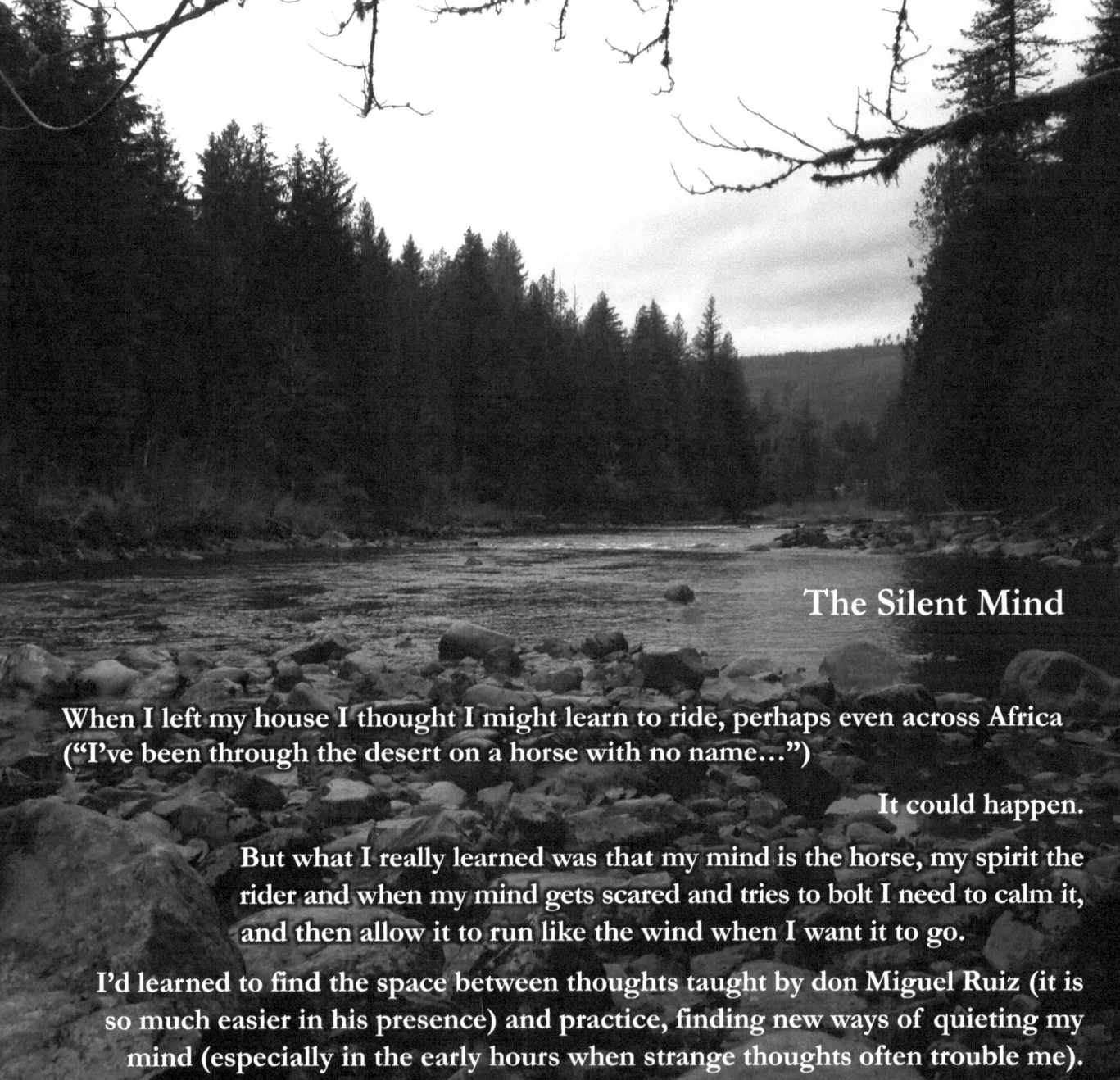

The Silent Mind

When I left my house I thought I might learn to ride, perhaps even across Africa ("I've been through the desert on a horse with no name…")

It could happen.

But what I really learned was that my mind is the horse, my spirit the rider and when my mind gets scared and tries to bolt I need to calm it, and then allow it to run like the wind when I want it to go.

I'd learned to find the space between thoughts taught by don Miguel Ruiz (it is so much easier in his presence) and practice, finding new ways of quieting my mind (especially in the early hours when strange thoughts often trouble me).

The first step is awareness.

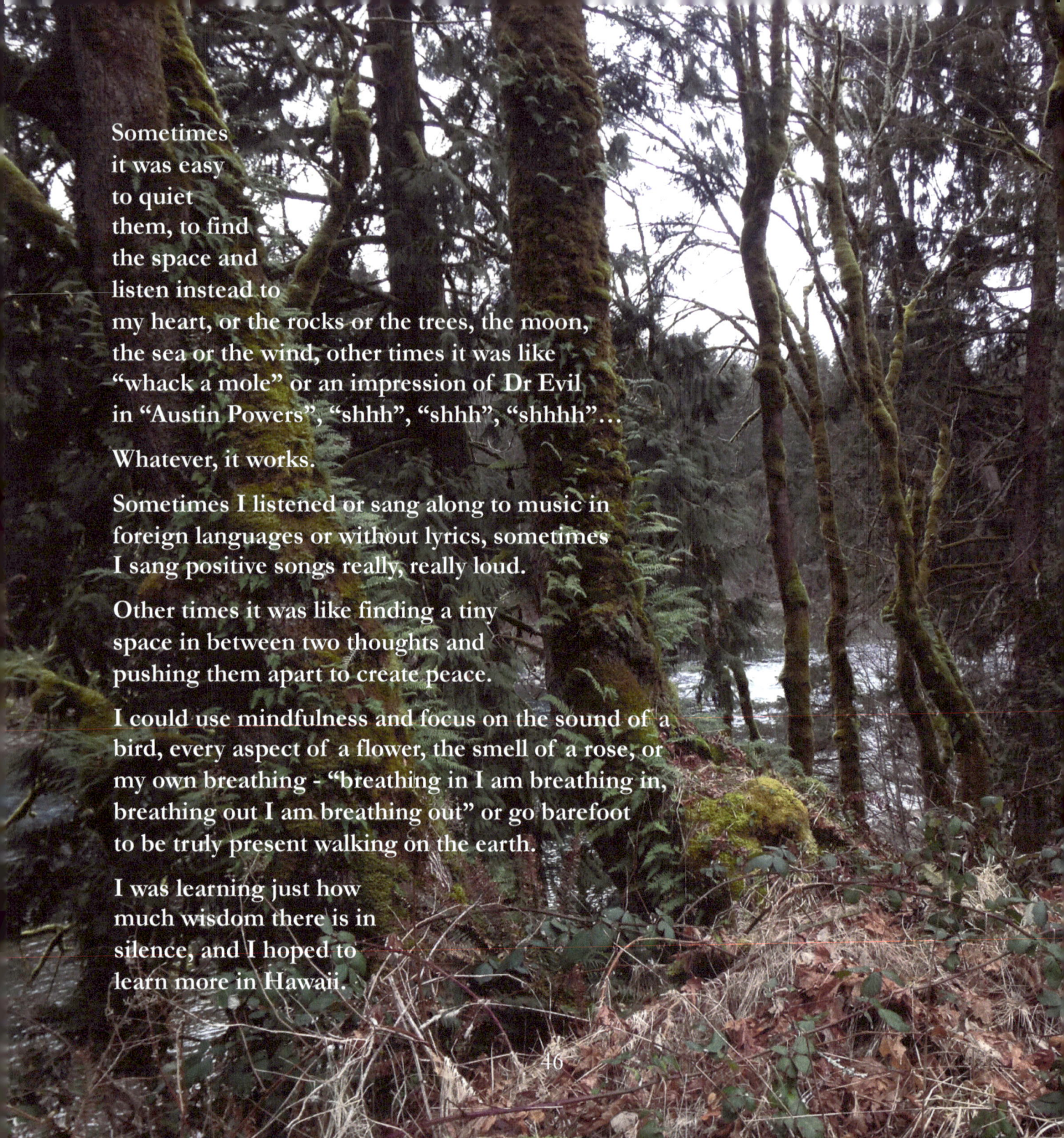

Sometimes
it was easy
to quiet
them, to find
the space and
listen instead to
my heart, or the rocks or the trees, the moon,
the sea or the wind, other times it was like
"whack a mole" or an impression of Dr Evil
in "Austin Powers", "shhh", "shhh", "shhhh"…

Whatever, it works.

Sometimes I listened or sang along to music in foreign languages or without lyrics, sometimes I sang positive songs really, really loud.

Other times it was like finding a tiny space in between two thoughts and pushing them apart to create peace.

I could use mindfulness and focus on the sound of a bird, every aspect of a flower, the smell of a rose, or my own breathing - "breathing in I am breathing in, breathing out I am breathing out" or go barefoot to be truly present walking on the earth.

I was learning just how
much wisdom there is in
silence, and I hoped to
learn more in Hawaii.

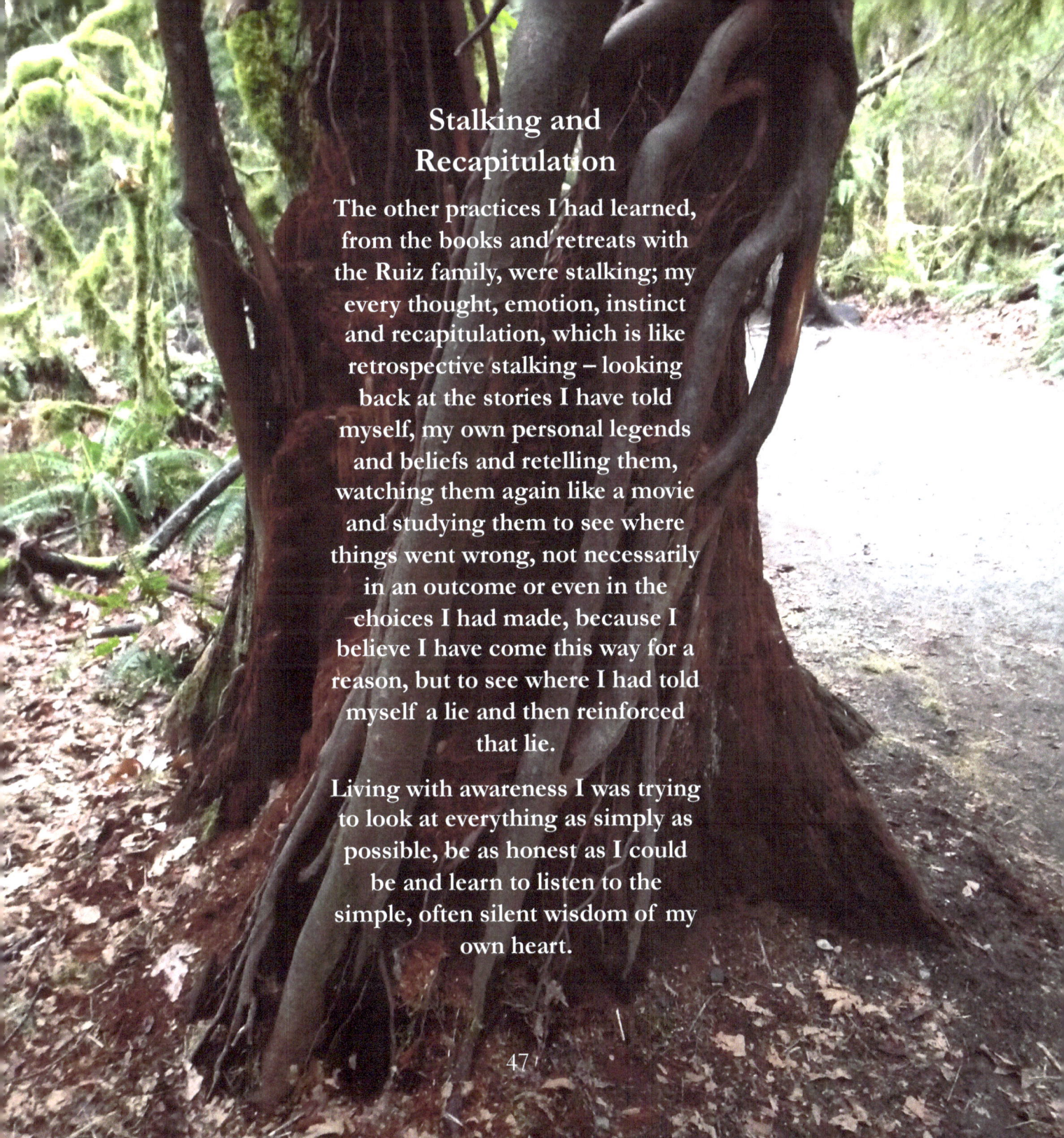

Stalking and Recapitulation

The other practices I had learned, from the books and retreats with the Ruiz family, were stalking; my every thought, emotion, instinct and recapitulation, which is like retrospective stalking – looking back at the stories I have told myself, my own personal legends and beliefs and retelling them, watching them again like a movie and studying them to see where things went wrong, not necessarily in an outcome or even in the choices I had made, because I believe I have come this way for a reason, but to see where I had told myself a lie and then reinforced that lie.

Living with awareness I was trying to look at everything as simply as possible, be as honest as I could be and learn to listen to the simple, often silent wisdom of my own heart.

Death Is Just An Illusion
Separation Is Just An Illusion

The only "death" is living death – suffering.

Every life is perfect, so why do I feel bad, feel sad, that you are not experiencing this with me?

Why do I feel lonely not being with my family, loved ones or just watching my favourite show?

Because I am, alone, listening to myself, no distraction, changing, metamorphosing and it is sad and challenging and wonderful and letting go of parts of myself and grieving.

It is okay, it is perfect, to open up; my heart, my hands and everything and I will become exactly what I am.

There's a hotel overlooking Snoqualmie Falls, but I don't want to stay, it makes me sad, so I tear round Washington State, heading towards Anacortes, wondering if I have time to get on a ferry tonight.

It's dark so early, I pull over on an industrial estate looking at hotels on my phone and finally feel the pull to

The Wild Iris Inn in La Conner

The place is heaven sent but there's no way I'm eating the cookie they've left out for me, uncovered. The owner warns me 7pm is too late to get dinner here, apart from in one little bar with an open fire – where the waitress asks me if I've tried the famous Wild Iris cookie – the best in the world. Across the water I can hear Native American drums.

I have learned to listen to my hosts, so I turn on my underfloor heating early (mistakes made on my Camino in Spain). The bath is superb, and made better by taking a cup of tea and my Wild Iris cookie in with me. The bed is one of the best in the world, and in the morning I have to drag myself out of it. Then I am up and off, to Anacortes, (where I see deer eating people's front gardens), to the ferry to the San Juan Islands, with my timetable, so I know at just what time I need to find a bed or my way back to the ferry terminal. First stop is Orcas Island where I want to check out the Doe Bay Resort, they have yurts.

I finally get bored of ferries (which I thought was impossible) riding from Anacortes to **Orcas Island**. But the drive is stunning, and, as I'm turning round a bend on the road it hits me again so hard it knocks all the air out of me. "Derek's dead."

But it's also my brother, grieving for him, the life we lost when he had a stroke. I have to pull over and walked down to the shore and breathe. It's also my ex, accepting it's over. As I look out I know the only way to get to acceptance, to stop grieving, to stop being in pain and suffering is to accept it, accept them, accept myself exactly as I am.

And I see so clearly, even now, my decisions to go somewhere, do something, perhaps even staying in a yurt, it's trying to be cooler, more exciting, as if somehow, if I can impress my ex he'll change, want to be with me again.

Doe Bay Retreat

But the yurt feels like me, so I book it, paddle for a brief moment on the shore here (it is very cold) and then visit their spa, which is clothing optional and everyone sits in the grubby hot tub complaining. So I go make up my yurt, not only with the bedding supplied but also with my silk liner and Puffy.

I have my car here if it does get too cold, and the cosy kitchen stays open all night. I spend the last of the daylight making up my weird veggie dinner and watching the shore and the animals, before curling up in my yurt, freaking out about the cold, and the fact the only other people in the whole resort seem to be the ones next door.

Turns out the fire here doesn't give out much heat at all, but I am just warm enough to sleep. In the night I have to get up and walk across the site to the bathroom, there's no moon or stars, it's just very, very cold. But somewhere in the very early hours something true comes to me, which is that I can work anywhere, so as dawn approaches I get up, make tea in the kitchen, and sit out on the bay and work on my books as I wait for dawn.   (And when it gets too cold I can go into the yoga studio and wait for dawn in there.)

I am thinking of all the stories told by my mum and my grandparents about when she was young, when they came from England, first to Canada and then the US, as they moved around, him working for different companies, when they were always heading off to camp in the wilds, or to skate over frozen ponds in Canada.

How brave they were, packing four children, plus a mother and a little brother and all their belongings into a car and heading off, and what adventures they had.

A Place Has An Energy Or A Personality, A Style

What I realised, sleeping in LaConner, was that we attribute so much to people's behaviour, to environmental factors, to it being "downtown" but there is more at play here.

In Seattle I can feel the kindness of downtown, the goodness of the city as a whole, and it draws good natured people, it feels like me before I became more disciplined. It's like the woman in "Breaking The Waves", like the little mermaid giving everything for love. But it's the kind of energy that works like an enabler, giving, giving, giving... These are the kind of places, like Sedona, where the Native American people did not build homes. It's a sacred space perhaps, for vision quests or cleansing or healing, but a transitional space. I felt it in Granada, that if I didn't leave, use the energy as a boost to get on my Camino it would become addictive, and the same in Porto, these are the places where I started; the beginning and the end days of my Camino de Santiago.

As I pulled out
of the orbit of Seattle I felt better,
excited to be going, to be moving.

I was sad in Snoqualmie, maybe
because the native people can't do
their rituals here the way they used to.

I thought of Nachi Falls in Japan,
of talking to the goddess there,
it's just energy, but it's also life.
In Hakone I couldn't sleep because
of the energy of the brook running
past me, it was meant to be
restful but nature in Japan
ran me ragged talking
to me, waking me up.

In Spain I rested in the treehouse and
I could feel new energy rushing into me in Granada and in Porto. It's these
places that people, hippies, the homeless congregate, because of the energy.

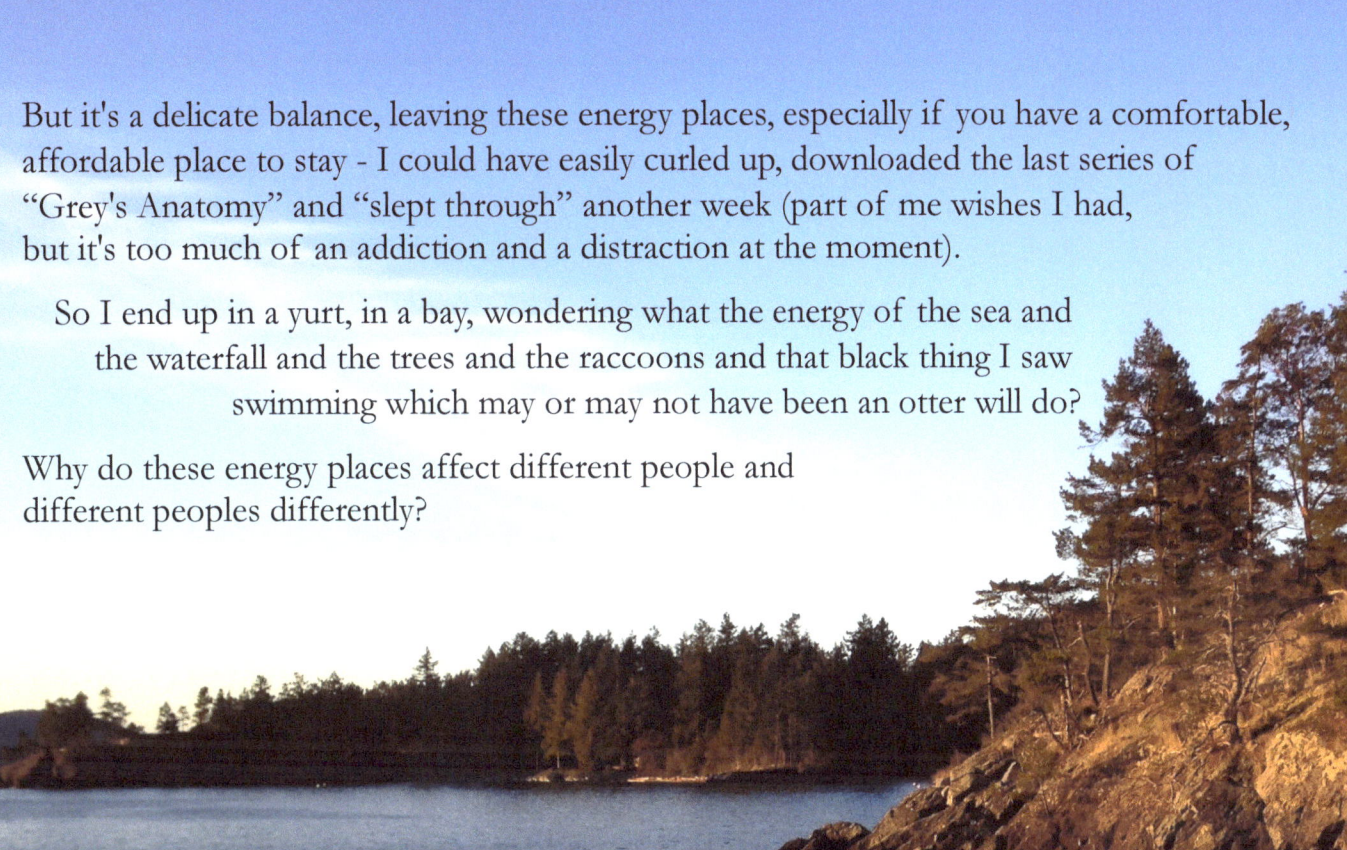

But it's a delicate balance, leaving these energy places, especially if you have a comfortable, affordable place to stay - I could have easily curled up, downloaded the last series of "Grey's Anatomy" and "slept through" another week (part of me wishes I had, but it's too much of an addiction and a distraction at the moment).

So I end up in a yurt, in a bay, wondering what the energy of the sea and the waterfall and the trees and the raccoons and that black thing I saw swimming which may or may not have been an otter will do?

Why do these energy places affect different people and different peoples differently?

Why do some people get addicted to alcohol or other substances?

Maybe it's genetic or growing up getting used to it, certainly there are Spanish gypsies who've lived for generations in the sacred mountain in Granada, but other people will tell you that if you stay for too long it'll drive you mad.

Mount Constitution

I throw everything in my car and am off, just after sunrise to see the view from up high, rated as one of the best views in the world according to another piece of paper I picked up from the rack on the ferry (where I found out about Doe Bay). I talk to locals who tell me they've never come up.

"How long have you been here?"

"Three years."

It's my advantage, living in the space of travelling fast, I may not be here tomorrow, I may not pass this way again. Carpe diem.

The Olympic mountains are clear in the distance, and I keep heading higher.

The snow finally stops me, I have to park and hike a little. I pay for my permit and then realise perhaps I wasn't supposed to put the cash in the little box. I don't go too far, just circle round in the woods, to see the view, something is calling me on.

I rush on to the ferry with moments to spare, and on to San Juan Island, and another whale museum.

San Juan Island

It's very interesting.

They tell me to forget about seeing orcas.

It's very, very beautiful here but I'm frustrated trying to figure out where I'm going, how I'm going. Now I finally have a car I discover a passenger ferry from Seattle to Victoria BC where one of my retreat friends lives. I'm trying to get to Canada, but none of the ferries from Anacortes run in the winter.

I feel like every which way I turn is blocked, I'm just going to have to go back and drive up to Vancouver.

What's even more annoying is that as I walk up the coast Vodafone keeps messaging me "Welcome To Canada!"

I'm so close.

I'm not so patriotic that I need to see English Camp, but I read in another ferry magazine that it has one of the world's oldest Bigleaf Maples (it used to be the world's biggest until it got damaged by a storm).

A war was almost fought over the killing of a pig, but the English and American camps instead sat opposite each other while they figured out who the San Juan Islands belonged to.

In the end they decided the US, without a drop of blood (apart from the pig's) being spilled.

If it had been the English I would already be in Canada.

So close.

I hug the tree, which is bursting with light, love, and friendship.

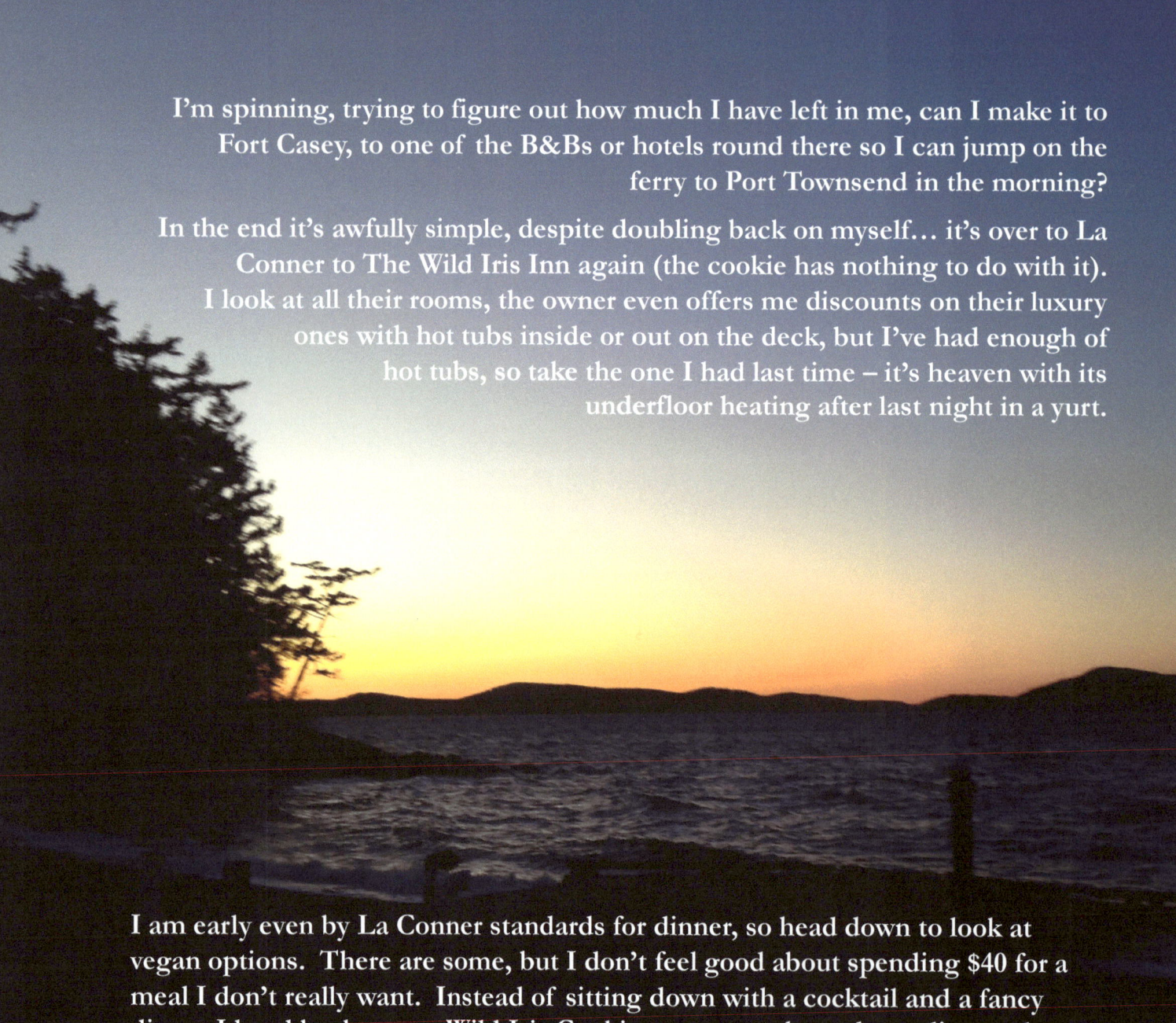

I'm spinning, trying to figure out how much I have left in me, can I make it to Fort Casey, to one of the B&Bs or hotels round there so I can jump on the ferry to Port Townsend in the morning?

In the end it's awfully simple, despite doubling back on myself… it's over to La Conner to The Wild Iris Inn again (the cookie has nothing to do with it). I look at all their rooms, the owner even offers me discounts on their luxury ones with hot tubs inside or out on the deck, but I've had enough of hot tubs, so take the one I had last time – it's heaven with its underfloor heating after last night in a yurt.

I am early even by La Conner standards for dinner, so head down to look at vegan options. There are some, but I don't feel good about spending $40 for a meal I don't really want. Instead of sitting down with a cocktail and a fancy dinner I head back, to my Wild Iris Cookie, to my snacks and supplies, and eat well and sleep even better, ready for the next day.

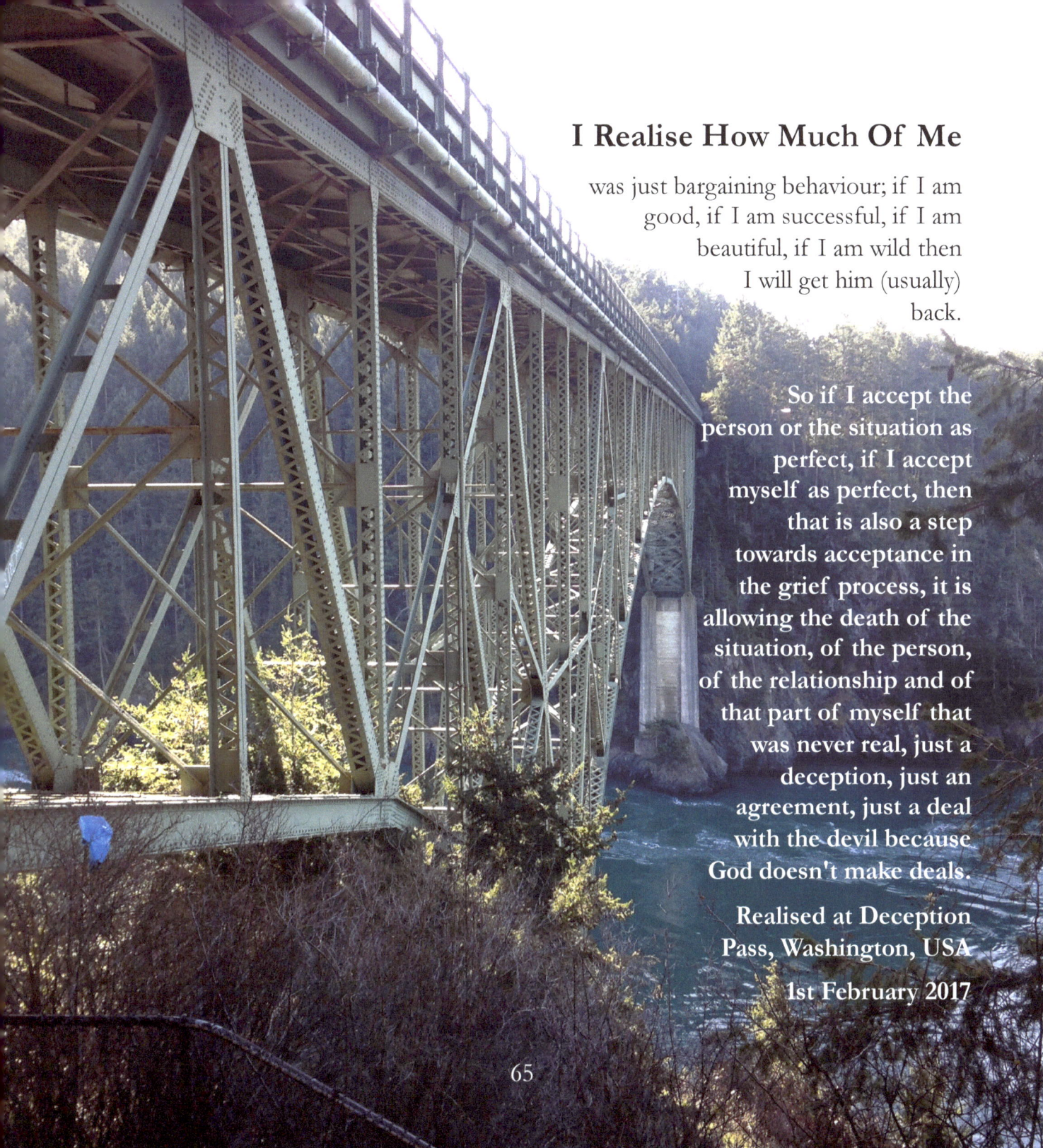

I Realise How Much Of Me

was just bargaining behaviour; if I am good, if I am successful, if I am beautiful, if I am wild then I will get him (usually) back.

So if I accept the person or the situation as perfect, if I accept myself as perfect, then that is also a step towards acceptance in the grief process, it is allowing the death of the situation, of the person, of the relationship and of that part of myself that was never real, just a deception, just an agreement, just a deal with the devil because God doesn't make deals.

Realised at Deception Pass, Washington, USA

1st February 2017

How Could I Ever Get Tired Of Ferryboats?

This is the journey from Fort Casey to Port Townsend. It's an hour and ten minutes and I stand out on deck for almost the whole time, drinking in the views.

I am following up some leads I found in onboard magazines and the racks of local information guides. I have discovered a Native American museum in Suquamish on the North East side of the Olympic peninsula, not too far from Bainbridge and the penny has finally dropped that Forks is a real town, where "Twilight" is set, and when I found the mention of a hotel on the beach at La Push, run by the local tribe - the Quileute, well, it sounds almost too good to be true (and at around $50 it's in my stay forever budget).

So the plan is to head west off the ferry, over to La Push, to First Beach to see if it's somewhere I could stay. I still like the idea of holing up for a few days to write and catch up with myself. Then perhaps head south to check out the Hoh Rainforest.

It takes much longer than expected. At first the drive along the water, lakes and sea on my right is stunning, but I soon get bored. I'm muttering "I'm bored, I'm bored, I'm bored…" in my head when a bald eagle swoops down right beside me and steals a fish. I'm in shock and so not bored any more.

It may also take longer because I stop at every Twilight sign along the way to take pictures, and also at more traditional cultural places like the Native American art galleries, but I get there.

And they have rooms. Overlooking the beach, with its giant driftwood. She can't show me as they're being cleaned, but I can choose one which even has its own kitchen, it's so easy my head is spinning.

I take a walk along the beach to clear it.

I've found it, the perfect spot to sit and write. I sit down and watch the sun.

And my spirit says. "Okay we found it, let's go."

"WHAT!!!!"

But I can't deny it, deny what my heart is telling me – it's time to go. Onwards and upwards it calls. I get back in the car, in disbelief at my self and head on down. I slide through Forks, which as Meyer's books describe isn't much to look at, but the beaches are spectacular all the way down the west coast as the sun slowly sets.

I race past the Hoh Rainforest, it's going to get dark soon and so I can't go into the woods. I'm flying, it's dark and I need to find gas, which I do in the tiniest little gas station that's about to close, and then it feels like just a few moments later I hit Aberdeen and breathe a sigh of relief.

It's hard to stop anywhere and part with any money after finding such a perfect set up in La Push, but eventually I know I have to pause. So I wander into one chain hotel, Marriott perhaps, where I can't bring myself to spend $150 on a basic room, so head on down a little further to Elma where I part with $80 for a standard room with half decent toiletries, a comfy bed, a crappy processed breakfast and zero sound proofing. I'm up before the sun and pushing through, with no idea what my plan is.

And then I see it. Mount Baker, aflame.

This, I think, is why I drove so fast around the Olympics, if I hadn't I would never have seen this.

I follow my instincts, (and the satnav) heading towards the Suquamish Museum which won't even be open yet (and then on, I'm feeling "Go to Canada.") I am badly in need of a decent breakfast after my plastic waffles. I turn left and find myself outside a diner. It has to be good; the Coastguards are coming out laden with cartons.

Turns out its specialty is vegetarian breakfasts.

"How did you find us?" asks the owner.

"I just followed my heart." (and my stomach) I say.

I have everything, including biscuits and vegetarian gravy (that's American gravy not English gravy, oh forget it, let me show you.)

Tastes a lot better than it looks.

I'm so excited to finally visit a Native American museum, hoping to learn about traditional healing, about the sacred places and rituals, and this place, the Suquamish Museum is unusual, it's clear it's been the work of so many, to celebrate, to curate and to honour the heritage of these people.

I am gutted. Because as I learn about the culture I learn something unexpected. This tribe had slaves. And the slaves were considered another class or caste of people. Even if they could make enough money to buy themselves out of slavery, which they did in order to carry on living with the families who owned them, they were never considered equals.

Something changes in me when I read this. I've held traditional wisdom so high, especially Native American, for so long. It was the Thoachta treatment at Aji Spa that freed me, helped me to release so much I'd been pushing down.

I didn't believe everything Belen told me at Aji, I'm used to allowing space between me and my healers; we are usually of different religions. But this was something different, it echoes something don Miguel Ruiz says, that the Toltecs stopped teaching, hid their wisdom because it was being abused. There is so much corruption in spirituality. An idea becomes a belief and then a rule, a wall, a prison. When the concept of reincarnation becomes so powerful that people start to believe someone born poor, disabled or in a different place is being punished for their previous life, when a system with hundreds of levels of grading ourselves as humans can exist.

I guess the penny had never really dropped for me before that, as well as all the beauty and healing magic in indigenous culture, there is so much bullshit.

I wander near the museum, it really is a beautiful area, and I respect them for laying it all out, not trying to hide from their past, even if is dark and misguided.

And then it's back to Bainbridge, to that ferry that I love, and this time I'm driving off, through downtown and racing up onto the fast roads, the freeway, heading to **Vancouver**.

To the grumpiest immigration guy I've ever met. I don't have the visa waiver because the one place you don't actually need it in Canada is driving up from the States. He seems to take it personally. "How much money do you have in your bank account?" It seems a bit personal but I tell him how much I have in one account (you don't want to say too much money or they think you're trying to move in, too little and they think you might be a burden) and he nods. He asks where I'm staying, how long I'm staying, what I'm doing. My "I don't know"s do not go down well.

Once again I am berated for not having an onward flight booked, but he begrudgingly lets me into the country. I cross the border and pull over. I'm in Canada, now what?

I don't feel any sense of success or elation, if anything I feel worse. I walk into the small tourist centre (do I want to go skiing? The runs are lit up at night?) I change my Mexican pesos into Canadian dollars, it's a terrible exchange rate but the pesos won't be any use here. Back in the car I look on booking.com, all the places I like are back in the US, do I want to go back and risk the wrath of another border official? I drive to a small seaside town, perhaps this is it, but when I try to get a parking ticket the machine won't work and I look down to see an old condom on the floor. I book a "deluxe villa" up near the airport, I'll figure out my plan tomorrow.

The sunset is so spectacular, with the lights of the ski runs it's worth getting lost.

All The Way Round Seattle

I can't seem to get over Derek, McDreamy, Patrick Dempsey - I can't get over this character's death in "Grey's Anatomy", me who is telling everyone that they just need to grieve, allow in the pain of grief. I'm driving round a corner and I hit a pocket of grief and pain about my brother's accident, my ex being my ex, and I have to pull over, I try to let it go, but it still comes up.

I realise I have stopped watching the show, although I think it's terrible that so many people walked away from the show because of his death - boycotted it. Although I've had some big stuff going in my life and it's only just twigged I could download and watch it on my travels, have been fighting the urge to do so all the time in Seattle, I find the thought of the series moving on from there really, really hard. Every time I ride the ferry to Bainbridge I'm in tears. "Derek's dead."

Why am I so triggered by the death of a fictional character?

It's 11 years of watching, I tell myself, it's so many years being invested in this relationship, this happy ending and then it's over. I found my happy ending and it's over?

I go round and round, like worrying a tooth, trying to recapitulate as I've been taught, when did my story get twisted around?

I think I find it - my grandfather's death, that was so sudden. My mum's chemo, the thought that she will get sick again. All this time being in the States, even going to Canada, it makes them feel so big, makes me miss them so much, camping, being outdoors makes me think of him so much, being near the waves makes me miss him. The weather makes me miss them, I want to go home.

And I wake up feeling terrible in Vancouver. I want to go outside but my "deluxe villa" is actually a guest suite in a Chinese family's house (where the only person who speaks English is their young daughter) which I actually really like, but it's 5am and I don't feel I can go outside and wander round their garden. Plus it's freezing and the garden is a patch of green between houses, the most boring garden in the world. So I throw up, book my flight to Hawaii, and then I walk outside and it's snowing.

My body knew to go.

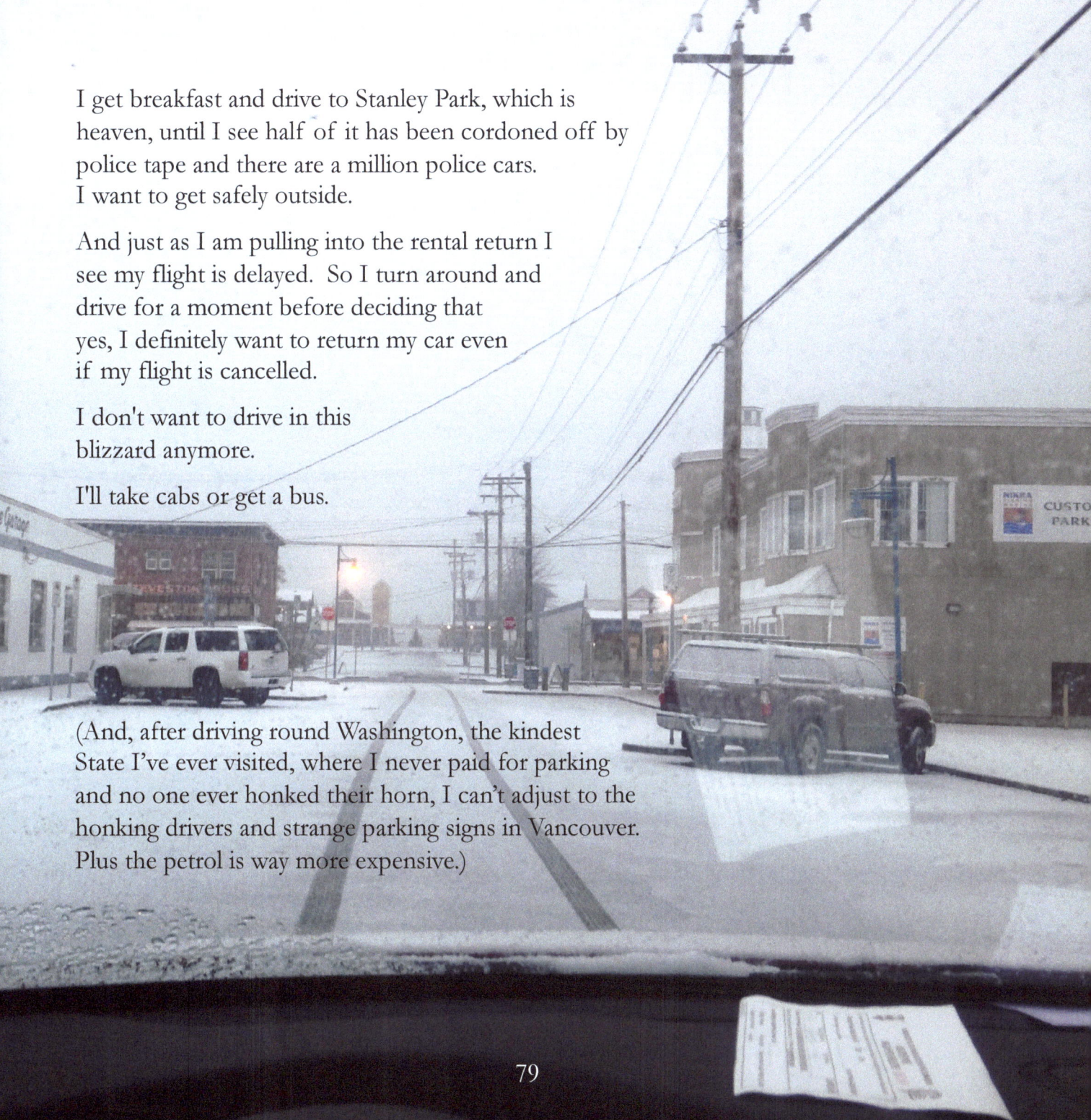

I get breakfast and drive to Stanley Park, which is heaven, until I see half of it has been cordoned off by police tape and there are a million police cars. I want to get safely outside.

And just as I am pulling into the rental return I see my flight is delayed. So I turn around and drive for a moment before deciding that yes, I definitely want to return my car even if my flight is cancelled.

I don't want to drive in this blizzard anymore.

I'll take cabs or get a bus.

(And, after driving round Washington, the kindest State I've ever visited, where I never paid for parking and no one ever honked their horn, I can't adjust to the honking drivers and strange parking signs in Vancouver. Plus the petrol is way more expensive.)

And I call my mum from the airport and I'm crying so hard, I miss her so much, and I know that I'm about to get on a plane to be on the other side of the world to her.

"I'm only a phone call away, only a day away on a plane." I say.
"I so wish you were with me."

"Oh" but she says "the next best thing to me going is you going and telling me all about it." So that's what I tell myself, even as I'm crying and we say how tired I am and she says "Just get yourself a hotel, don't worry about the money" because I'm saying how expensive it all is in Maui (which it is, but I've spent more on dumber stuff).

And I say "Tomorrow I'll call and tell you it was the best thing I ever did, I'm just tired and it's hard getting on a plane away from you, even though it's the right thing for me."

I am freaking out, feeling sick. The lady who checks my bag is so nice, she's shocked the border guy asked me how much money I had - he had no right. She tells me US immigration is inside the airport, so I will technically be in the States before I get on the plane. "Don't ever say you don't have a hotel booked". She tells me it was a murder in the park. She tells me to think only good thoughts, but I still have to go outside and sit on a bench and look at the snow, just as I did before I walked into the terminal.

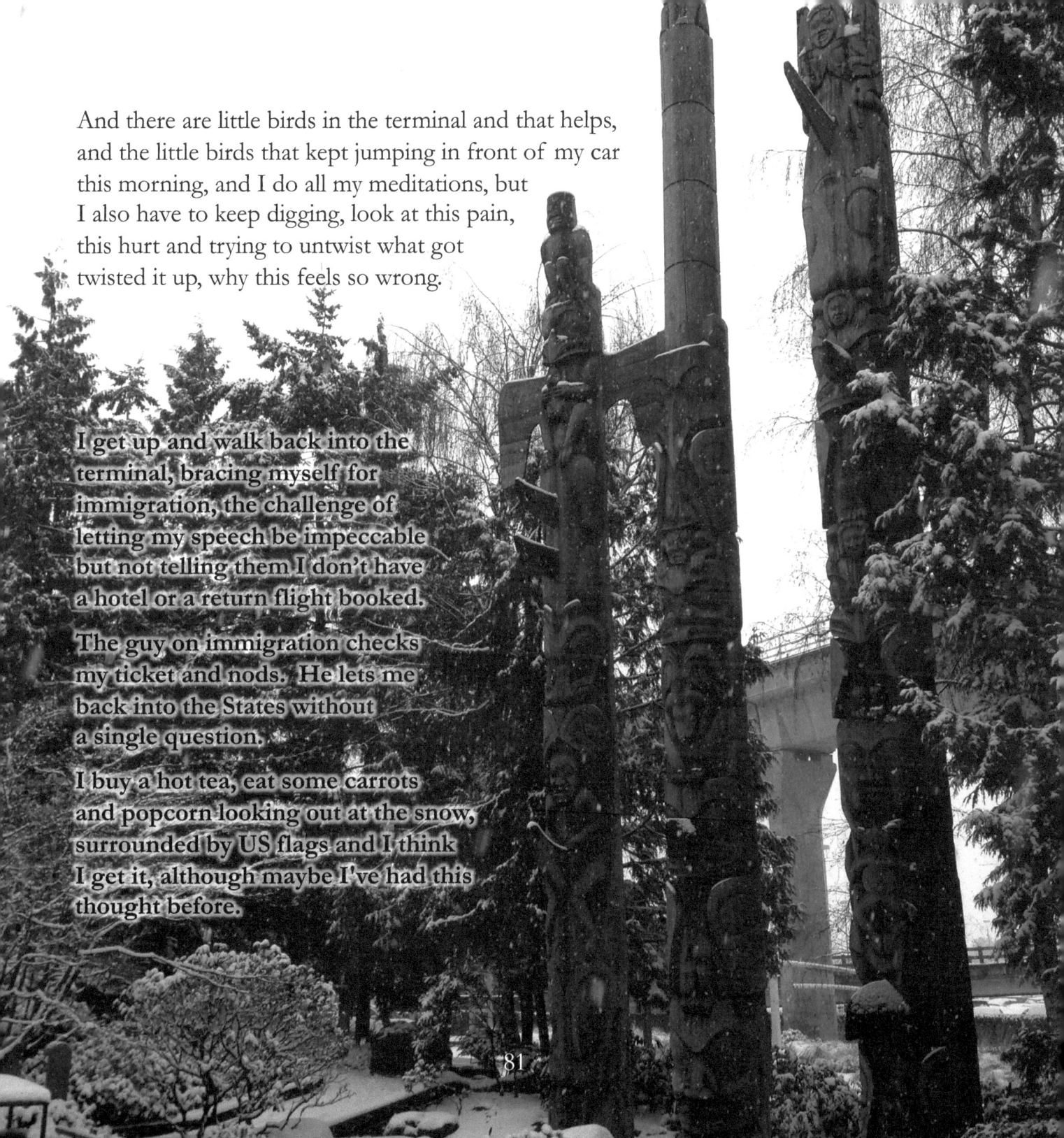

And there are little birds in the terminal and that helps,
and the little birds that kept jumping in front of my car
this morning, and I do all my meditations, but
I also have to keep digging, look at this pain,
this hurt and trying to untwist what got
twisted it up, why this feels so wrong.

I get up and walk back into the
terminal, bracing myself for
immigration, the challenge of
letting my speech be impeccable
but not telling them I don't have
a hotel or a return flight booked.

The guy on immigration checks
my ticket and nods. He lets me
back into the States without
a single question.

I buy a hot tea, eat some carrots
and popcorn looking out at the snow,
surrounded by US flags and I think
I get it, although maybe I've had this
thought before.

I moved to Paris when I was 23. Within a week my Grandad was admitted to hospital with suspected cancer. Luckily I had a return ticket because bizarrely it was cheaper than a single. I took the flight back, visited him and then we got the call; he wouldn't last the night. I was in the right place at the right time, there was nowhere else I'd rather have been. At his funeral there was standing room only as I said goodbye to the man who had tried to teach me to swim, to camp…

Just over a year later I got another call in Paris. My mum had been diagnosed with cancer, her doctor told her to put her affairs in order, she had less than six months. I realised of all the things I wanted to do in my life my biggest regret would be if I didn't spend more time with my mum. I moved back to England, even though the diagnosis turned out to be wrong. It wouldn't be the last time a specialist would tell her to prepare herself for her world to end.

The man who had been more of a father to me than my own, as he had to others. The man about whom I still hear stories, am still learning all of the many things he did for us before I can even remember, a great man.

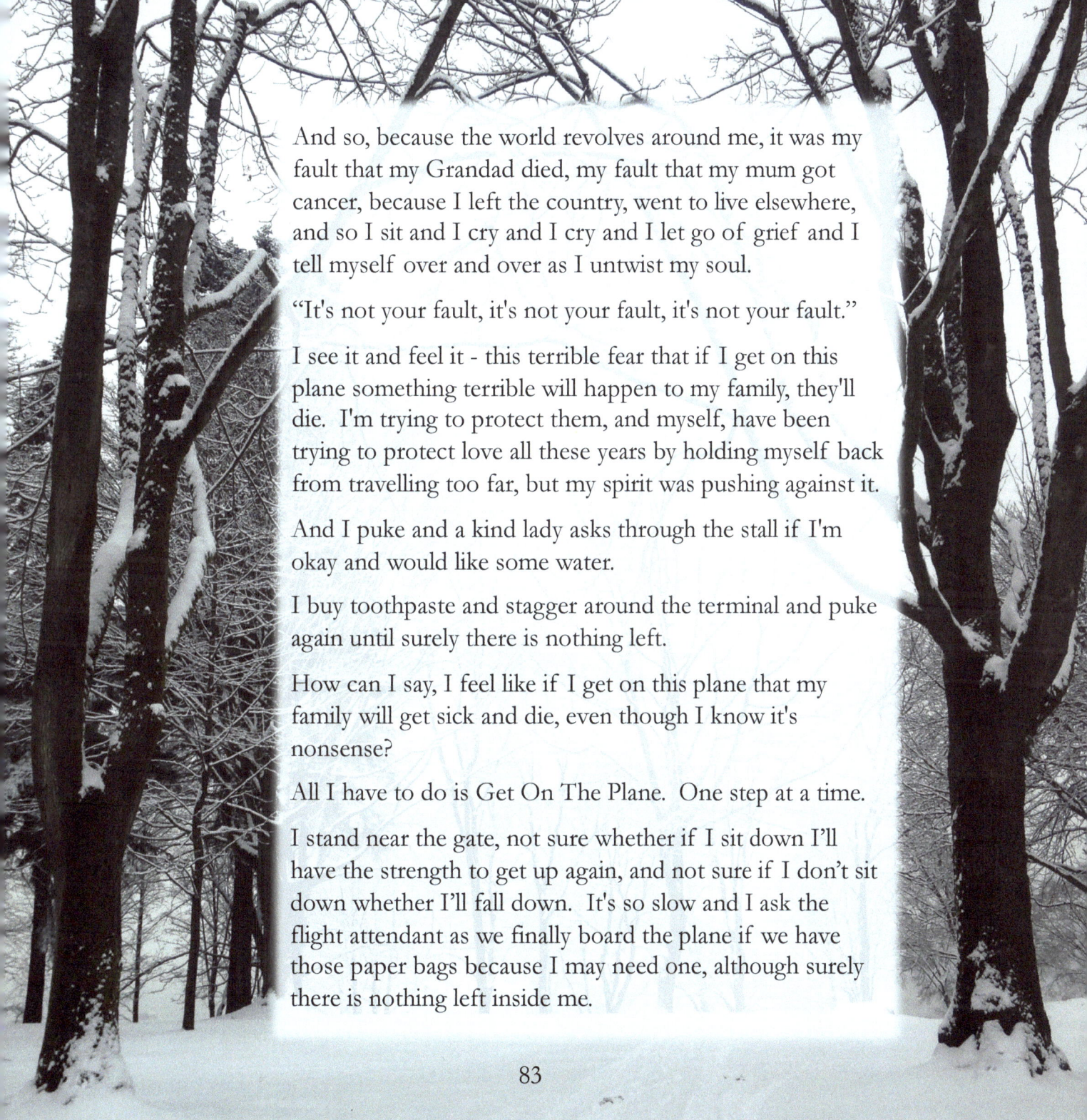

And so, because the world revolves around me, it was my fault that my Grandad died, my fault that my mum got cancer, because I left the country, went to live elsewhere, and so I sit and I cry and I cry and I let go of grief and I tell myself over and over as I untwist my soul.

"It's not your fault, it's not your fault, it's not your fault."

I see it and feel it - this terrible fear that if I get on this plane something terrible will happen to my family, they'll die. I'm trying to protect them, and myself, have been trying to protect love all these years by holding myself back from travelling too far, but my spirit was pushing against it.

And I puke and a kind lady asks through the stall if I'm okay and would like some water.

I buy toothpaste and stagger around the terminal and puke again until surely there is nothing left.

How can I say, I feel like if I get on this plane that my family will get sick and die, even though I know it's nonsense?

All I have to do is Get On The Plane. One step at a time.

I stand near the gate, not sure whether if I sit down I'll have the strength to get up again, and not sure if I don't sit down whether I'll fall down. It's so slow and I ask the flight attendant as we finally board the plane if we have those paper bags because I may need one, although surely there is nothing left inside me.

And I pray for help, I pray because it's a rough ride and my head is pounding, but I don't want to take my painkillers because I want to ride it out and because if they come back up it'll be even worse.

And I say "I am perfect and my life is perfect" and I Get On The Plane, and I tell myself that even if I die, even if they turn the plane around, I am going back to God, back to life, and if we don't fly I'm turning around and getting on the next plane back to England. I'll rent somewhere and write and download "Grey's Anatomy".

I tell myself this as the babies cry and the plane has to be de-iced and the boy behind me kicks my chair and God comes through for me and one of the only empty seats on the plane is next to me. (Or maybe telling the flight attendant I was going to puke?)

I cry and I snot and eventually after over an hour and a half of sitting on the plane, after the hour and half of the original delay I do vomit, just a little.

And then there's a delay because someone doesn't Get On The Plane (I don't blame them) and their bags have to be taken off.

I let go and I keep telling myself "It's not your fault, it's not your fault and it doesn't matter if I even get there, because just getting on the plane to Hawaii is the healing" I realise.

And just when I think we are finally going to take off, the pilot announces that he's not quite sure and wants to come back down and take a look at the wings. He walks down the plane to check, but he only looks at one wing and then goes back to the cockpit.

I am pretty sure we are all going to die.

And then we're taking off and I can undo my seatbelt and lie down across the spare seat under my Puffy blanket, bought in place of a sleeping bag in REI, and pass out.

A few hours later and I do take my painkillers and sleep for a few more hours and then I have to sit up because the seatbelt sign comes on, and I remind myself (because it's bumpy) that no one ever died from turbulence. And I put my feet up on the empty chair and snuggle in my Puffy and write this.

The final stretch into Maui itself is rough, but for me the worst is over and, as the kids scream at the turbulence, I am calmer than I have been for a long time.

Maui

Hawaii smells terrible, but at least it's warm. It's getting on for 2am by the time we land and I am in joy about getting off the plane, without a care in the world about my luggage or even where I'll sleep tonight. It'll all work out.

I have this idea that everyone who lands in Hawaii gets a lei, I may be wrong and I know it's late, but sure enough they're handing out leis to everyone. I stand there looking pathetic. "Didn't you get a lei?" says the guy in charge. I shake my head. He's intent on trying to fix it and I am impressed. Until he says "Are you part of our group?"

"What group?" I think it's a pharmaceutical conference. "Where are you staying?"

Turns out it's at least an hour away so I shake my head. I've just discovered something about Booking.com - as it's after midnight it won't show me any rooms for tonight – just tomorrow, because that's technically "tonight". I'm not too stressed, it's warm, I have my Puffy, I'm not dead, but I am really quite tired and it looks like the kind of small airport they'll actually close when they get rid of us, the last passengers.

I ask at the taxi stand because the tourist information is closed and they help me track down a local hotel, the Maui Beach Hotel, which, although it's $200 is not $300 like the Marriott. They say they'll hold me a room and I am deeply grateful. Then I try to get a cab. It's a long wait, it feels like there's just one lady working tonight, and I'm on my last legs as the people behind me ask me to please move my bags up the queue because the people behind them are getting ancey and I have a few words for them along the lines of "It's 2am, we're all waiting and we're not going to get there any faster if I move one foot along the kerb, you know I'm first and so does everyone else." Then I dump my bags and sit on the wall. I am doing my best. I even have it in me to turn round and say "Hey guys, is anyone going the same way so we can double up on cabs?" And eventually I give a ride to another couple (not the ones bumping me) who are going to the hotel with almost the same name next door. Luckily the cab driver tells us it's just the drains at the airport that are backed up – Hawaii doesn't really smell so bad.

It is on the beach. But it's more than $200 because they add in all the bastard US taxes and ridiculous things like "occupancy tax" which I always think is like adding an "eating tax" to your food. But I pay it. I kind of hate it. My room smells terrible. I can't settle. I can't open the window because my room is on the ground floor, the air conditioning unit is going nuts. I check and double check the sheets, which are pristine, I think if there was so much as a speck of dust I would complain or leave. Perhaps I am so wired because of the journey, perhaps I will wake up in the morning and love it here?

I doubt it when I see a roach in the hall near the kitchen, but it's just the one.

I walk along the dark beach and back to the patio where I bump into some people from my flight. (I think a great deal of us end up here, but everyone else has a plan for the next night – AirBnB is popular). These guys also hate the hotel, they don't want to go to bed either. They've decided to crack into their duty free and stay up all night. "Join us!" I'm tempted, but it's a slippery slope, although at least it's another option, which makes me feel better. I go back to my room, shower, get my period, and get into bed with my Puffy on top, my hands on my heart and manage to drift off to sleep. I've had worse.

It is beautiful, there's no denying it, but that's what I always say to my mum about a place that's not doing anything for me. "It's very beautiful."

But I am, as I keep reminding myself, in Hawaii.

I walk down to the beach for a swim
(the guys apparently did eventually go to bed).

It's a weird beach, and not just because the sand is so dark.

I walk around the cove and go to hug a tree, but it's a good thing I glance at it as it has a dead animal skinned and tied to it. That's a new one for me.

I walk back and see a guy making art with small pieces of driftwood, he tells me he's from Micronesia and that I am very beautiful.

I look up to see a wild eyed woman, I smile at her and she yells at me "What are you looking at?" She's hitting rocks out to sea with a stick, but now she aims them at me. Hawaii is not what I expected. There's also an angry man with two black dogs. So much venom right here (later people will tell me this is where the homeless people live and ugly rumours about the hotel).

I keep going, back past the hotel where I finally make it into the water and swim. I'm swimming in Hawaii. I look across the bay and see surfers. That's more like it.

And then a few teenagers are being instructed out to the water on a traditional Hawaiian boat. I am charmed and come up to ask their teacher or coach about it. He doesn't want to talk, perhaps they are just sick of tourists here.

I go back to the hotel and eat really good banana pancakes (not included in the price) and drink coffee with the woman who was drinking vodka and Baileys with her friends last night and asked me to join them. I thank her for giving me the option. We talk a lot and finally I help her with her takeaway coffees; she wants to get her friends moving to their rental place. They open the door in their underwear and are shocked to find me standing there. They're still drinking and have the TV on loud, it's a different life.

They say you attract people on a similar wavelength to you, or at the same vibration. In retrospect, because I took my migraine tablets I was technically high when I arrived in Maui. In that light my experiences make more sense.

I go on Booking.com in the cold light of day, book what looks like the nicest place in Maui regardless of the expense, (also it's the only hotel available for the next two nights) and wait ages for a taxi over to the Lumeria.

I am doing my best to take care of myself, to build myself up again, to eat well, sleep well and practice meditation and all the good stuff before I can even start to explore Hawaii. I am so tired from the journey that I do not even have the energy to get into the pool or the hot tub on my first day.

The food is incredible, breakfast is included, lunch is a buffet and dinner is family style, I book my vegan plate. There's some confusion about alcohol. When I check in they tell me there's no alcohol because it's a retreat centre, but as I walk into dinner they're pouring out glasses of prosecco. I decide to abstain and embrace the Buddhist vibe.

I won't leave for the next two days, I don't need to, on one side I can look down over the beach, the other the mountains. And it's stormy, the woman on reception tells me it's a Kona wind, which is unusual.

"What's a Kona wind?"

"A wind blowing up from Kona."
But there's more to it than that, she tells me when you set your intention during a Kona wind it has a lot of power, so be careful what you wish for.

I hug the trees, but they are grumpy, unwelcoming, it's like they don't want me there. It's okay, I find a friendly rock which is happy I am here. "Welcome to Hawaii."

All I want is to nap, but when I get into my room the sheets are torn and stained and I am not impressed. I trudge back over to reception where they promise to put it right. I also ask if there's a room on the other side, I'm feeling it more and I'm not sure about being on the corner, but in the end the only sound I hear is the wind.

I nap, listening to my relaxing music, trying to stay with the feeling that at least the rock wants me in Hawaii, I'm not sure about anything else.

It's so hard to get up when my alarm for dinner goes off, but so worth it for the food, even though it's too cloudy to see the sunset, and then I am back in bed for 8pm.

And slowly, as I recover from the exhaustion of letting go of that dark lie - that I was somehow responsible for the bad things that happened to my family because of my wandering off, the energy that I had been using to maintain that lie comes back to me.

I am in joy to be here, in Hawaii.

The Top Of The Mountain

As I sat on the top of the mountain at Lumeria in Maui I understood and felt the truth about what it is to love and be loved. I sat on the grass and meditated overlooking the sea and reached a point, a top of the mountain of feeling and being that was the highest I have yet experienced.

To try to put it into words is to describe a meditation of enlightenment with the words "We are all one". If, in just saying these words, we could understood and feel this deep truth, well, pretty much all the retreat and meditation centres, not to mention yoga schools, bars and spas would go out of business.

These are just words.

It is like me, standing now in Venice, telling you it's pretty, showing you my photographs, when I want you standing beside me, feeling the cold biting through your fingertips, the rush of hot coffee and Sicilian cannoli in your blood, the images of waterways burned into your retina as well as a hot pocket full of iPhone snaps.

I want you to know what it is to wander dark streets,
see black gondolas smacking against the waves in the shadows,
to see the night reflected in tiny dank canals that hold no comfort
before the dawn, when thoughts turn to bodies dropped out of windows
and figures shrouded and masked for carnival, to know what it is to walk and
find yourself in the right place all but for a few yards of canal with no bridge and
to know you need to shoulder your bag, your life and retrace your steps back to where
you took a wrong turn.

To feel the energy of a thousand artists honouring beauty, feel their passion for life till it makes you dizzy and a thousand murderers and ghosts that wake you up before dawn playing with your darkest fears.

This is Venice.

It is as far removed from the Venice of Las Vegas as your whole life and every breath you ever took from your last ID snapshot.

I will try.

I believe it's important and many of my teachers have tried to explain it to me, I have tried to learned it over and over, each time getting closer and closer to this moment. As Mother Theresa said "There are things that cannot be seen or touched but must be felt with the heart."

I sat and meditated on the life of my beloved.

I had felt, travelling to Hawaii, the deep lie at the bottom of so many of my fears, of my refusals - like a horse refusing to jump when I could so easily have soared.

I felt deep acceptance of myself just as I was in that moment.

I've heard that acceptance of a death comes when we can see it, not as a life interrupted, but as a life completed.

I could see our relationship as complete because of where it had brought me, but I could only arrive at this moment by accepting my life, his life and the relationship as perfect.

The butterfly had metamorphosed from the caterpillar, crawling through the most painful and messy period of transition, of meltdown and being both less and more than a single being and then become a thing of lightness and joy.

I could see his life and him, not as something to be fixed or corrected, but as perfect, I could feel that every step he took was perfect.

This is love.

To see each other; our most precious soulmate and the stranger smoking or drunk on the street, and in the same way we can know "We are all connected", we can know "They are perfect and every step they take is perfect." It is letting go in a way, but, more than holding on or letting go, it is finding a perfect balance, pona if you will, of holding a person in our heart without in any way trying to change them. Because we would be trying to improve on perfection.

It would be like paving Venice or fixing every battered shuttered window or straightening the canals, or covering the sky and painting it a perfect sunny fresco like a Vegas Venice.

And it is sharing ourselves, our dark, our light, our stories with them when our heart tells us, without judgment, without fearing that our words might overbalance them. It is not trying to protect them from us.

Because this is another dark lie that fucks up our lives.

When I went to visit the grey whales in Baja it was without too much thought, on my bucket list was already "gorillas in Rwanda" but my ex had been going to work with orangutans in Borneo before he died. Why was it not on my list?

"I don't want to go and see orangutans in Borneo." "Do I?"

And so I recapitulated, went back through my life and found where the wiring went wrong. In a zoo, when I was little, looking into the eyes of an orangutan in a little white box and feeling the terrible
pain of being locked up,
feeling that living death.

What could I do to help, or indeed to help the polar bear pacing backwards and forwards? Leave them alone. Don't visit zoos, don't harass animals. Of course I want to see orangutans in the wild, in a refuge, I just don't want an animal to be put in a box so I can visit.

It was as if I told myself I didn't want to see Venice in case I made it sink more.

When I smell pollution, cleaning chemicals or smoke, or even when I imagine I do, I hold my breath. I breathe shallow. I don't give it my full lung. I hold everything together waiting for the perfect air. And in so doing I hurt my lungs, I hurt my ribs and my back which is held rigid and, as everything is connected, soon my neck is hurting and pain even starts to shoot through my head. Yes, I need to get out of that shitty air as quick as I can, but I still need to let my body breathe, because in holding my breath, trying to protect myself, I hurt myself. Isn't it crazy, that I should have to learn to breathe again because of how I have hurt myself through fear?

Isn't it crazy how people have to learn to eat again after hurting themselves with food, through fear? We can use anything, even our breath as a way to heal or a way to hurt ourselves. Because the real demon is not food or air or alcohol - it is fear.

And the most important thing I have to learn, to relearn is how to love. Myself and others.

I turn to my loved ones and love them. I feel it and see it as the top of what I have been taught is love. I love them… And then when that love starts to curdle - to turn to… "I love my Grandma… but I worry that…" I stop myself. I stay in the pure love, I let go of worry and fear and remind myself "She is perfect and every step she takes is perfect."

I could write down all of the worries and fears I am avoiding, but why?

It is enough to just… stop. To stay in love.

To stay on this side of love, the side that trusts, the brave side, and not to slip to the fearful, protective side that wants to control, that wants everyone I love to be what I want them to be.

Love without judgment.

Without pity.

Without abuse.

Without shame.

Without fear.

Without neediness.

And in that moment looking down off the mountain (literally) at the shore I set my intent, knowing how careful I have to be because it is a Kona wind. I have everything I need and have finally discovered what it is to love and be loved, so my only desire now is to serve the universe. And then I go for a nap.

Ha

I had hoped to heal my lungs in Hawaii, and just before I arrived I read an article about what the "ha" in Hawaii means. It relates to the breath, our every breath. When we think of the first breath every human takes we see what a miracle it is. Then one day we will breathe our last ha, our last breath, and that last breath will be so precious, but what we forget is that every single breath we take is just as precious as the first, or the last.

So I worked with my ha, with my breath, breathing into my body, to the areas of my lungs I had been depriving of movement and right down into my soul, finding a new breath, a self loving breath that did something wonderful to my whole being.

It reminded me of something from the movie "Hitch", that my best friend treasures; "Life is not about the number of breaths you take, it's about the moments that take your breath away."

That afternoon I practised my breathing, my "ha" lying on my bed. With clean air blowing through the screens on my window, I used the techniques I learned for free diving - I did breath ups, breathing two thirds of the way into my lungs, holding, releasing, holding (some call it square breathing, it's in many yoga practices), several times, being so calm, letting all my adrenaline die down, disengaging my brain so that even that required the least amount of oxygen, until I was almost inert, and then in that moment, when I felt I was ready, I took the biggest breath of air I possibly could, breathing down to every dark neglected place of myself, using the breath as a way of loving myself exactly as I am. And it was amazing, and then when the breath had gone all around me, held as long as I could, I let go and recovered, just lay there letting myself pant and stop thinking about controlling anything, because this is recovery (at least in free diving).

And then I had to get up and close the windows because the wind was battering the shutters too loudly.

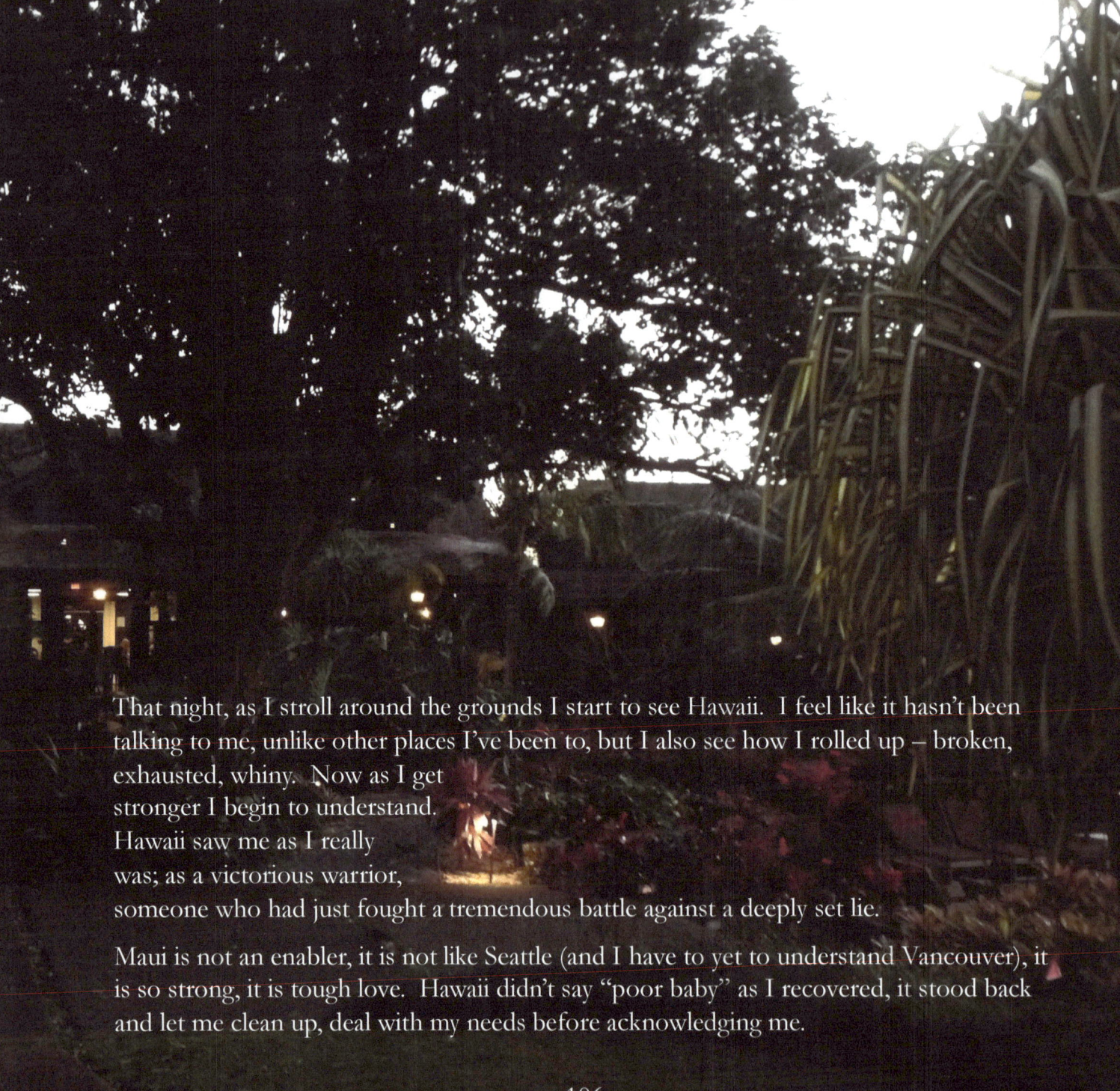

That night, as I stroll around the grounds I start to see Hawaii. I feel like it hasn't been talking to me, unlike other places I've been to, but I also see how I rolled up – broken, exhausted, whiny. Now as I get stronger I begin to understand. Hawaii saw me as I really was; as a victorious warrior, someone who had just fought a tremendous battle against a deeply set lie.

Maui is not an enabler, it is not like Seattle (and I have to yet to understand Vancouver), it is so strong, it is tough love. Hawaii didn't say "poor baby" as I recovered, it stood back and let me clean up, deal with my needs before acknowledging me.

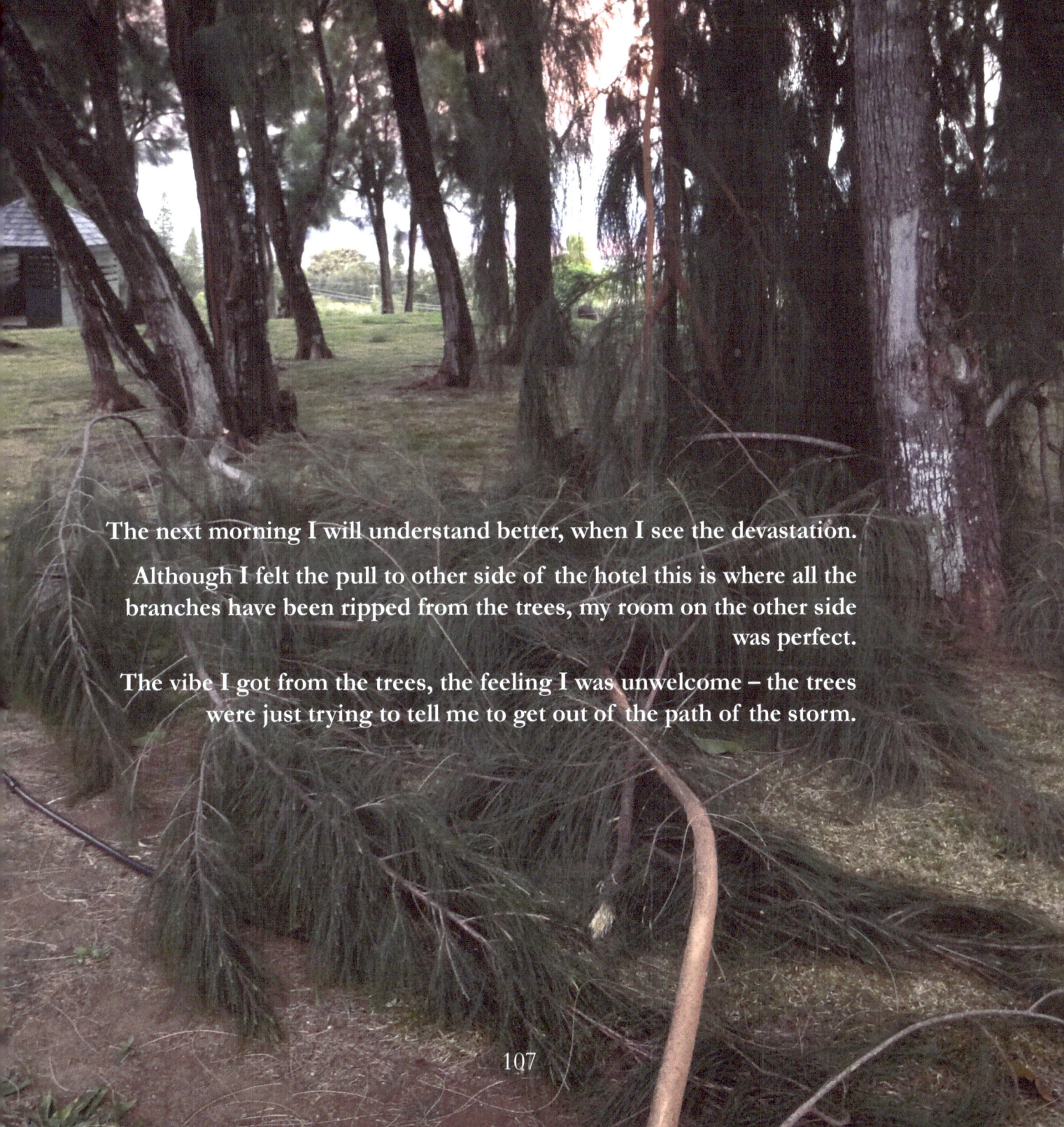

The next morning I will understand better, when I see the devastation.

Although I felt the pull to other side of the hotel this is where all the branches have been ripped from the trees, my room on the other side was perfect.

The vibe I got from the trees, the feeling I was unwelcome – the trees were just trying to tell me to get out of the path of the storm.

I Let Go

Of all my warm clothes, my fleece, and the things I've not worn so much.

I let go of my make up as I've not worn it since New Year, and toiletries because I'm sure I'll find them along the way.

I want the lightest possible pack to wander round Hawaii.

Somewhere Over The Rainbow

It's time to leave. I am rested, well fed, have spent hours in the hot tub even though I never got round to having a massage and I have cleared out my pack – gifting my warm army surplus trousers (which are filthy as I wore them all round the States) to the waitress who says she is ready to leave Hawaii after 22 years (it seems to be going around).

I love that at breakfast when I spy a rainbow over the mountain it was the most natural thing in the world to run in and shout "There's a rainbow" and for most of the people to come out to look. This is my kind of place.

A lady and her husband stand and watch with me. "Thank you for telling me about the rainbow. My little granddaughter has been so ill, we didn't think she would survive but what helped her was rainbows. She said whenever she saw a rainbow it meant everything was going to be alright. I don't know where she got it, but it's going to be alright."

It's time to find my "pona" or balance. It's funny, I've listened to Israel Kamakawiwo'ole's "Wonderful World" a million times, but now I understand what he's talking about. We all got to find our own "pona", no one else can do it for us.

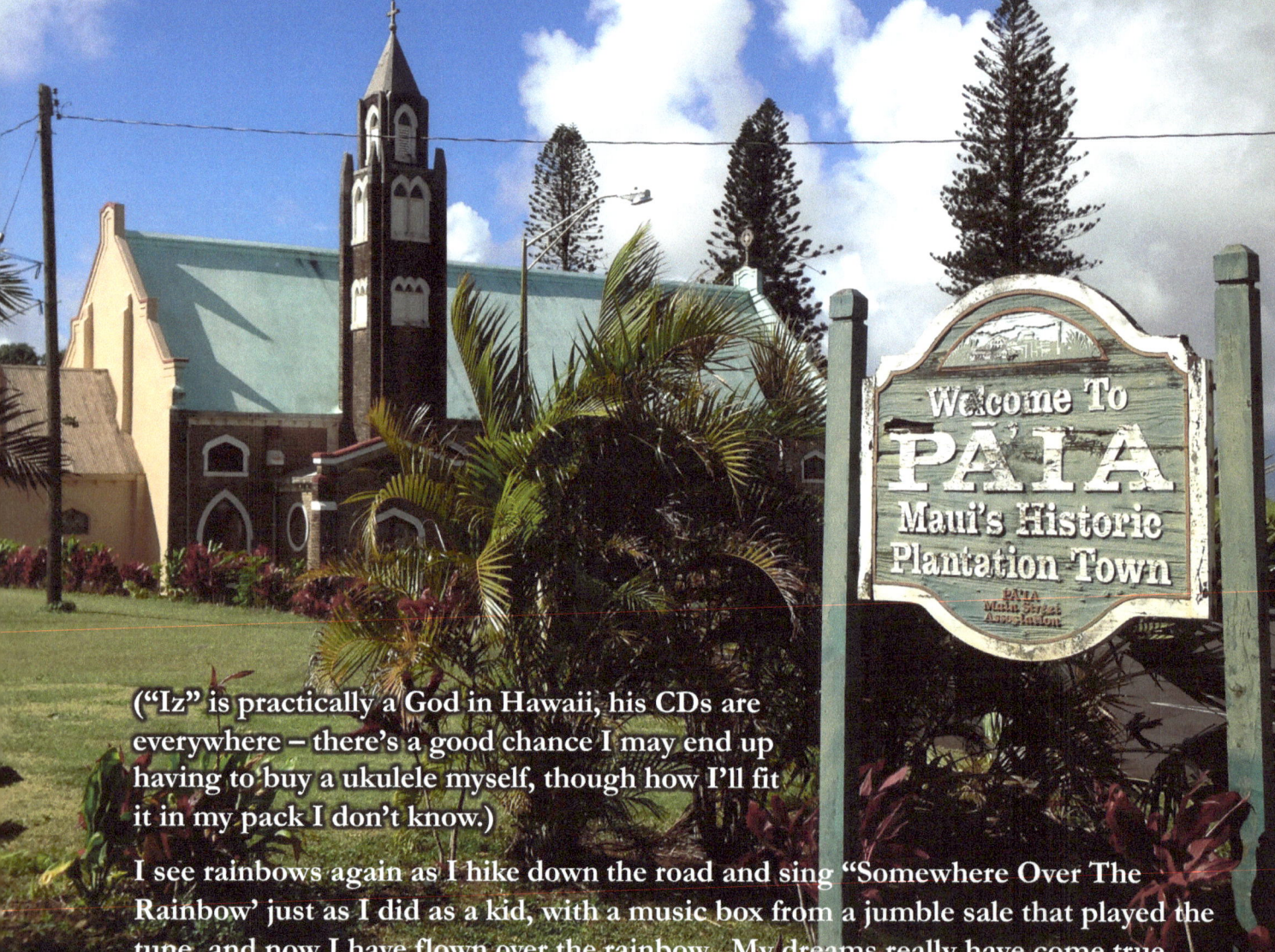

("Iz" is practically a God in Hawaii, his CDs are everywhere – there's a good chance I may end up having to buy a ukulele myself, though how I'll fit it in my pack I don't know.)

I see rainbows again as I hike down the road and sing "Somewhere Over The Rainbow' just as I did as a kid, with a music box from a jumble sale that played the tune, and now I have flown over the rainbow. My dreams really have come true.

I walk into town and call my mum as I wander about. I walk to a beach where the locals offer me some booze and I see turtles climbing up on the beach for a nap and start to plan where I'll go, what I'll do… fly to another island, stay in another guest house…

And it all… leaves me cold.

So I backtrack, call the whale watching people to find out about tours, because that's really the only thing I want to do in Hawaii (and Maui is the best place to see humpbacks). And then I book my lovely Lumeria hotel again for tonight, and look at flights back to London, and get an Uber back to the hotel (because someone tells me that yes, it does work in Hawaii).

I love the hotel even more now, can see how beautiful it is. And I sit on the meditation platform, where I didn't sit before, because it really is a big deal to come home from here, so I need to be sure it is where my heart is leading.

And it's as true as it's always been - there really is no place like home. And I walk the labyrinth, each turn seeing the beauty of the place again, perhaps like I need to keep turning and returning to my family to see things clearly.

And when I hug a tree this time it speaks clearly:

"We just want you to be happy."

I am happy.

Happy to see my friends at the Lumeria, to eat the fabulous food, to get up before dawn and be picked up by the hotel's driver in his super tech car.

Happy when he offers to give me a massage in the back of the car, and takes off his shirt, my bra and gives me a hug. (This is Hawaii.) But also happy to book an Uber on to the airport because I'm not sure I want to repeat the experience.

Happy to be on a whale watching boat again (this time with coffee and a loo aka "head").

Happy when we see the first whale breach, and when they tell us that humpbacks wave and I feel free enough to stand on deck and wave energetically like a four year old at the whale waving to me across the water.

Happy when I get coffee and feel the urge to run back on deck just as a humpback not only breaches, but twirls like a true "gymnast" as they are nicknamed, almost onto the boat. (It's the closest our guide has seen them.)

Happy when they drop the mike… into the water and we hear the male whale song and understand that they sing it to each other to gather so the females will find them more appealing as a group (I have learned a lot about the mating behavior of whales this year – it's an eye opener.)

…wait, what do you mean you didn't see the whale wave. Wait a second…

And I learn that the water around Hawaii is the closest to the true colour of water because nothing grows in it, but the water around Seattle is dark grey because there are so many nutrients.

Don't Wait
(Part 2)

Don't wait for the people you love to give you what you want, what you need. It's hard enough to figure out for ourselves what that is - it's not fair to put the burden on them to figure it out.

So many people are waiting for the right person to come along to start living their life.

People were surprised when I bought my flat, my boyfriend was upset "It's like you're just getting on with your life, making a plan without me." which surprised me - it wasn't about him, I just needed a place to live. But so many of us are waiting, expecting someone else to come along and give us our happy ending.

You are the love of your own life, take what you need.

In the airport I was learning that "Aloha" means so much more, Hawaii still had so much to teach me. "…for some of us it is more than a greeting, but rather a life force that defines who we are and why we are here."

A   Akahai – meaning kindness (grace), to be expressed with tenderness;

L   Lokahi – meaning unity (unbroken), to be expressed with harmony;

O   'Olu'olu – meaning agreeable (gentle), to be expressed with pleasantness;

H   Ha'aha'a – meaning humility (empty), to be expressed with modesty;

A   Ahonui – meaning patience (waiting for the moment), to be expressed with perseverance.

A secret of "Aloha" is that a person cannot do one of the principles without truly doing all and if you are not doing one you are not doing any. So to live "Aloha" is to be living all of the principles."

I felt like I was leaving just as I had woken up to Hawaii.

It was like the last time I saw my ex, after a week together he realised he still loved me. So often we only see things clearly as they end.

So I drank the good Hawaiian coffee in Starbucks (it was really, really good), I bought chocolate covered macadamia nuts, and most importantly a sweetly scented, fresh orchid lei for my mum, the best present I could ever bring her, apart from me.

Aloha is more than a greeting or salutation. It is a condition, a way of life, a mind set and an attitude.

Aloha is an action, not a reaction. It is a natural response of respect, love and reciprocity, and not a contrived series of motions or expressions that have been rehearsed and perfected for a commercial expectation.

Aloha is to be in the presence of life, to share the essence of one's being with openness, honesty and humility. It is a way of being, a way of behaving, a way of life. It is a commitment to being real. It is a commitment to accepting others and giving dignity to who they are and what they have to offer.

Aloha is not a slogan, pitch line or monogram. It is a spiritual principle that conveys the deepest expression of one's relationship with oneself, the creative and life-giving forces, one's family and community, and with friends and strangers.

"To gain the kingdom of heaven is to hear what is not said, to see what cannot be seen, and to know the unknowable – that is Aloha. All things in this world are two, in heaven there is but One."

Queen Lili'uokalani (1917)

Photo Credits

All photos by Pearl Howie and helping hands on her iPhone.

About the Author

Pearl has released herself back into the wild after living for 22 years in Wimbledon (give or take a couple of years in Paris and Southampton).

She is trying her best to be vegan.

She loves you and all animals, but is still working on practising unconditional love for bugs, and roosters and dogs that wake her up in the night.

She loves having adventures and being a spiritual warrior but, sometimes when she finds a nice hotel she will stay in bed and sleep all day.

She is hoping soon to go lie on a beach all day with a book.

It could happen.

Anything is possible.

Staylist

Sleep Inn, Seattle Airport, around US$100 including free shuttle to and from airport and standard American plastic breakfast (which you are welcome to take back to bed, according to their guest information), banana pancakes, (or was it waffles?) in bed with hot coffee brewed in my room, yes please. Booked direct.

(Not stayed due to pot issues) Green Tortoise Hostel near Pike Place

The Roosevelt, 1531 7th Avenue, Seattle Central Business District, Seattle, WA 98101 - US$121 not including breakfast (via Booking.com)

Quiet, clean and comfortable room, 115 Northeast 125th Street, Northgate, Seattle, WA 98125 – US$65 including coffee, full kitchen, shared bathroom, laundry room and parking (via Booking.com)

The Wild Iris Inn, 121 Maple Avenue, La Conner, WA 98257 - US$129 including breakfast (via Booking.com)

Doe Bay Retreat, around US$85 with out of season discount for yurt (and two day use of the spa and facilities) booked direct on arrival – no breakfast

(Not stayed but stunning location) Quileute Oceanside Resort, La Push from US$60

Stay Beyond Inn & Suites, 800 East Main Street, Elma, WA 98541 – around US$80 including cardboard breakfast

Canyatt House, 4475 Steveston Hwy Richmond BC, V7E 2K4 - CAD$75 – no breakfast but they let me use the kitchen to cook my weird dinner (via Booking.com)

Maui Beach Hotel, 170 W Kaahumanu Ave, Kahului, HI 96732 – around US$200 plus taxes not including breakfast

Lumeria Maui, 1813 Baldwin Ave, Makawao, HI 96768 – around US$450 per night including all taxes, breakfast, lunch and dinner (via Booking.com)

Book References and Further Reading

"The Four Agreements: Practical Guide to Personal Freedom",

"The Mastery of Love: A Practical Guide to the Art of Relationship",

"The Voice of Knowledge: A Practical Guide to Inner Peace"
– Don Miguel Ruiz and Janet Mills

"The Fifth Agreement: A Practical Guide to Self-Mastery"
– Don Miguel Ruiz and Don Jose Ruiz

"My Good Friend the Rattlesnake: Stories of Loss, Truth, and Transformation" – Don Jose Ruiz and Tami Hudman

"Happiness - Essential Mindfulness Practices" – Thich Nhat Hanh

"Wild" – film

Twilight series of books - Stephenie Meyer

"Grey's Anatomy" – TV Series – created by Shonda Rhimes

"No Mud, No Lotus" – Thich Nhat Hanh

"The Big Blue" - film

"Whale Rider" - film

"Eat, Pray, Love" – Elizabeth Gilbert

"Breaking The Waves" – film

"Austin Powers: International Man of Mystery" – film

"The Wizard of Oz" – film

"A Horse With No Name" – America - song

www.ingramcontent.com/pod-product-compliance
Lightning Source LLC
Chambersburg PA
CBHW041123300426
44113CB00002B/44